"With conciseness, clarity and proper nuance, James Papandrea offers an excellent primer on the developing christologies of the second century and shows their practical significance and implications on soteriology and anthropology."
Helen Rhee, associate professor of history of Christianity, Westmont College

"Papandrea has done a great service by producing this accessible guide to the early Christian controversies about Christ. He avoids simply dismissing some views as 'heretical,' but instead shows how these views grew out of a desire to emphasize some aspect of Christ's identity. Yet he also provides an explanation of why the majority church decided on the position it did. I would recommend this book to anyone wanting to gain a better understanding of early Christian theology and by extension the historic creeds of the church."
David L. Eastman, associate professor of religion, Ohio Wesleyan University, book review editor, *Journal of Early Christian Studies*

"*The Earliest Christologies* is a clear, accessible introduction to five common views from early Christianity. Papandrea offers a helpful taxonomy that avoids oversimplification. By placing Logos Christology within a spectrum of Christian attempts to express the faith, the author shows how orthodox Christology compares with—and ultimately surpasses—its various dialogue partners. With constant references to primary texts that are in turn supported by astute commentary, this book is an excellent starting point for any attempt to learn what early Christians believed about Jesus."
David Wilhite, associate professor of theology, Baylor University

"This is simply the best, most elegant and most lucid account of orthodoxy and heresy in early Christianity."
Mike Aquilina, author of *The Fathers of the Church* and *The Witness of Early Christian Women*

"James Papandrea eloquently introduces readers to dissident images of Jesus in the second-century church. Many groups wrestled with the question 'Who is Jesus?' and came to diverse conclusions. In this book, Papandrea helpfully sets out their views and asks what motivated them and why they (inevitably) failed to win the backing of the mainstream church. All in all, an excellent introduction to forms of 'other' Christianity and the whole discourse of early christology. A lively, readable and informed introduction to christologies deemed to be heretical."
Michael F. Bird, Ridley College

D1288079

THE EARLIEST CHRISTOLOGIES

FIVE IMAGES OF CHRIST IN THE POSTAPOSTOLIC AGE

JAMES L. PAPANDREA

IVP Academic

An imprint of InterVarsity Press
Downers Grove, Illinois

InterVarsity Press
P.O. Box 1400, Downers Grove, IL 60515-1426
ivpress.com
email@ivpress.com

InterVarsity Press® is the book-publishing division of InterVarsity Christian Fellowship/USA®, a movement of students and faculty active on campus at hundreds of universities, colleges and schools of nursing in the United States of America, and a member movement of the International Fellowship of Evangelical Students. For information about local and regional activities, visit intervarsity.org.

Scripture quotations, unless otherwise noted, are from the New Revised Standard Version of the Bible, copyright 1989 by the Division of Christian Education of the National Council of the Churches of Christ in the USA. Used by permission. All rights reserved.

Cover design: Cindy Kiple
Interior design: Beth McGill
Images: Christ in Majesty, © Odessa Fine Arts Museum, Ukraine / Bridgeman Images

ISBN 978-0-8308-5127-0 (print)
ISBN 978-0-8308-9972-2 (digital)

Printed in the United States of America ∞

Library of Congress Cataloging-in-Publication Data
Names: Papandrea, James L., 1963- author.
Title: The earliest Christologies : five images of Christ in the postapostolic age / James L. Papandrea.
Description: Downers Grove : InterVarsity Press, 2016. | Includes index.
Identifiers: LCCN 2015050890 (print) | LCCN 2016001644 (ebook) | ISBN 9780830851270 (pbk. : alk. paper) | ISBN 9780830899722 (eBook)
Subjects: LCSH: Jesus Christ—History of doctrines—Early church, ca. 30-600.
Classification: LCC BT198 .P365 2016 (print) | LCC BT198 (ebook) | DDC 232.09/015—dc23
LC record available at http://lccn.loc.gov/2015050890

P	23	22	21	20	19	18	17	16	15	14	13	12	11	10	9	8	7	6	5	4	3	2	1
Y	35	34	33	32	31	30	29	28	27	26	25	24	23	22	21	20	19	18	17	16			

This book is dedicated to

my brothers from other mothers,

the men whom I call my lifelong friends and

who continue to inspire me to be a better man:

Mike Aquilina, Joe Dilillo, Joe Groshek, Paul Jarzembowski,

George Kalantzis, Graziano Marcheschi,

Glenn Murray and Rich Vetrano.

As iron sharpens iron, so man sharpens his fellow man.

Proverbs 27:17

CONTENTS

Acknowledgments

This book (or, in fact, my career) would not have been possible without the people who taught me church history and gave me a love for the church and her tradition. I especially want to thank my first church history professor, James E. Bradley of Fuller Theological Seminary, and my dissertation advisors, Dennis Groh and Robert Jewett of Garrett-Evangelical Theological Seminary. I would also like to thank my colleagues and students at Garrett-Evangelical for their support and trust, as well as my research assistant, Kay Hardiman, who helped with the subject index.

Five Images of Christ
in the Postapostolic Age

As long as the apostles were alive, they were the ultimate authorities in the church, primarily because they had been disciples
of Jesus, or in the case of Paul, they could at least claim to have been
commissioned and sent by Jesus himself (Gal 1:1; cf. Acts 9:1-19). The
apostles, along with their own disciples, were the world's leading ex-
perts on who Jesus was because they had known him personally or
because they were there in Jerusalem when the Holy Spirit proceeded
to the church on Pentecost. And when they wrote the documents that
became the New Testament, they were (and still are) believed to have
been inspired by God. According to tradition, John lived the longest,
living into the early second century. But by the late first century, any
apostles still alive functioned like bishops with itinerant ministries of
oversight and regional authority. This means that the beginning of the
"postapostolic age" (the age right after the apostles) began at different
times in different places.[1] In Rome it had begun after the deaths of
Peter and Paul in the mid-60s of the first century. In Asia Minor it did
not begin until the death of John.

Therefore, while admitting that there is no clear or uniform beginning to the postapostolic age, we can still define it as the earliest
time in the church's history when there were no living apostles to give

---

[1]On the postapostolic, or subapostolic, age, see James L. Papandrea, *Reading the Early Church
Fathers: From the Didache to Nicaea* (Mahwah, NJ: Paulist Press, 2012), chaps. 1–6.

a definitive answer to the question that Jesus had asked: "Who do you say that I am?" (Mt 16:13-18). Human nature being what it is, the emergence of the postapostolic age meant that it was probably inevitable that there would be disagreements among the remaining Christians over even the most important aspects of Christian belief.

Although they had the New Testament writings, the church was still coming to a consensus on which of the early documents would be included in the canon.[2] This means that certain teachers or factions within the church could gain followers by ignoring or excluding those books of our Bible with which they did not agree. Some even edited the documents, cutting whole sections out of individual documents, including the Gospels. And even when there was agreement on the acceptance and authority of a particular text, there was often disagreement on the interpretation of that text—a phenomenon that continues to this day, as anyone who has ever had an argument over theology knows. In other words, two people can be reading the same passage of Scripture and understand its message differently. For example, what did Paul mean when he wrote to the Christians in Colossae that Christ was "the firstborn of all creation" (Col 1:15)?[3] Did he mean that Christ was the first created being? Or that Christ was the agent of creation, as we read in the first chapter of John's Gospel? Questions like these led to disagreements about the person of Christ in the early church. These disagreements can be categorized as five distinct views of who Jesus Christ was and is.

THE AIM AND SCOPE OF THIS BOOK

"Christology" is the name we give to what we believe about Christ. It includes beliefs about his personhood, his nature (divine? human? both?) and in what way he is a Savior or mediator between humanity and the divine. In an apocryphal document known as the *Apocalypse of Adam*, there is a description of thirteen kingdoms, which are allegories for thirteen different theories of who the Savior is—thirteen

---

[2]See ibid., chap. 6, "The New Testament Canon."

[3]Note that Paul was probably actually quoting a preexisting hymn in this passage. See James L. Papandrea, *Trinity 101: Father, Son, Holy Spirit* (Liguori, MO: Liguori, 2012), 33-38.

christologies.[4] The point that the author of this document was making is that all thirteen theories were wrong and only the fringe group that produced the document had the right answer. But the truth is that most of these christologies are variations of the same few or misunderstandings of the beliefs of other factions within, or on the edges of, the church. There were, in reality, five main christologies in the postapostolic age.

Most studies of early heresies, especially gnosticism, focus much of their attention on their speculative cosmologies, that is, their elaborate systems of many deities and angelic beings inhabiting ever-increasing numbers of "layers" within the heavens. The teachings of the excommunicated heretics are then described as salad-bar composites of paganism and astrology with elements of Christianity. This is because the primary sources that are available to us describe them that way, and there is no good reason to believe that their descriptions are not accurate. However, the early Christian writers who describe the heresies focus so much on the speculative and superstitious nature of their paganized version of Christianity (or their Christianized version of paganism) that they often don't tell us a lot about what they believed *about Christ* specifically. This book will set aside the cosmologies, and even the theologies (whether they were polytheistic, for example), of the early factions within the church and focus on their christologies—drawing out what they believed about the person of Jesus Christ, as far as we can know. Then we will address the relationship of christology with soteriology (salvation) and also its relation to lifestyle.[5]

We will limit our study to the postapostolic age, which for our purposes means primarily the second century, though with some overlap into the first century. And because we will not venture very far into the third century, I am not including modalism ("modalistic monarchianism") among the early views of Christ in the subapostolic age.

---

[4]Nicola Denzey Lewis, *Introduction to "Gnosticism": Ancient Voices, Christian Worlds* (Oxford: Oxford University Press, 2013), 239-41. Note that the thirteenth "kingdom" seems to be the author's attempt at describing Logos Christology, the christology of the mainstream (majority) church.

[5]For the connection of christology to soteriology (salvation), see Papandrea, *Trinity 101*, 67-73.

Modalism is more a phenomenon of the third century, and it is also technically more of a trinitarian heresy than a christological one.[6] However, I will address it briefly in the concluding chapter in a section on the later legacies of the early christologies.

Before going on, a word on the concept of heresy is in order. The terms *heresy* and *heretic* come from a Greek word that implies a faction—a person or group that departs from the majority or the accepted norm. Therefore, by definition, the heresies are those views of Christ that deviated from, and opposed, the view of the "mainstream" or majority of the church. It is true that often in the course of history it is only after a debate is settled or an ecumenical council is held that the heresy can be defined in contrast to the approved interpretation. It is also true that the interpretation of the majority of church leaders is usually the one that wins the day. However, this is not the same thing as simply saying that the story is written by the winners. There was a "mainstream" or majority church in every generation, and the heresies were those teachings that moved far enough away from the mainstream to catch the attention of the ecclesiastical authorities and generate a debate. We also have to remember that *all* of Christianity was an illegal, persecuted religion in the postapostolic age, so this is not a time when imperial power was used to discriminate against heretics, nor was it a time when heretics were executed for their teachings. That did not happen for another thousand years.

Having said that, I will use the terms *heresy* and *heretic* as little as possible in recognition of the fact that the "heretics" were probably sincere believers who thought souls would be at stake if their opponents won the day. And this is precisely what all of the proponents of every christology believed. They could not take a "live and let live" approach to christology because they all believed that the wrong christology would not save its believers.

We have to keep in mind that all five of these approaches to the person of Jesus Christ were options *within the church* in the postapostolic age. Even those that deviated from the majority were still

---

[6]For a general definition of modalism, see ibid., 77-79, and Papandrea, *Reading the Early Church Fathers*, 139-41.

within the church. If they were not, they would have been considered completely different religions rather than heresies. In any case, we can assume that people with different christologies worshiped together in the house churches of the late first and second centuries. And although there were certainly some "heretics," teachers of alternative christologies, who gained a following and created their own factions, the existence of different christologies does not necessarily point to completely separate communities.[7] In other words, we should not imagine these five christologies as representing five different "denominations" within Christianity.

In most cases, the alternative christologies probably grew up rather organically or around certain early teachers (whom we will meet below). At some time they attracted attention and sparked debate within the church, and if there was a faction leader, that person often got excommunicated by the bishop of the area in question. At some point, the factions made more of a separation from the mainstream and became, in effect, a separate sect. We may remember the words of John when he wrote, "They went out from us, but they did not belong to us; for if they had belonged to us, they would have remained with us" (1 Jn 2:19). When a faction moves far enough from the mainstream, it either leaves the church voluntarily or is kicked out—either way, it has gone beyond the boundary of what is considered acceptable by the majority, and therefore, by definition, it has left the church. This was especially the case with gnosticism as its syncretism moved it farther from Christianity until it finally became something other than Christian.

The Dilemma

The experience of the New Testament church, seeing the miracles of Jesus (and apostles who healed in his name) and especially seeing him after his resurrection, led to the worship of Jesus right from the beginning. Jesus was considered divine. However, the Gospels clearly attest to his humanity. He was born as a baby, grew up, felt emotions,

---

[7]Charles H. Talbert, *The Development of Christology During the First Hundred Years and Other Essays on Early Christian Christology* (Leiden: Brill, 2011), 26.

suffered and died. This means that when it came to defining what Christians believed about the person of Christ, those who wanted to emphasize his divinity had to at least address his apparent humanity, not to mention his suffering and death (even if to deny it), and those who wanted to emphasize his humanity had to address his apparent divinity and his unique relationship with God (again, even if only to deny it).

There were good reasons for being on both sides of this dilemma. Those who wanted to emphasize his humanity saw him as one of us and realized that if he were not one of us then it might mean that following his example was really impossible. Those who wanted to emphasize his divinity believed that people cannot follow his example perfectly enough to reconcile themselves to God and that salvation requires divine intervention.

Both sides—in fact every one of the five views of Christ—could agree that what humanity needs is a mediator to reconcile humanity and the divine and that Christ is that mediator. But they disagreed on exactly what it meant for Christ to be a mediator and how he would reconcile. This is in fact what creates the five views—five different ways of understanding how Christ is (or relates to) humanity and divinity.

DIFFERENT PHILOSOPHICAL ASSUMPTIONS

Part of what drives the five different answers to the question, "Who do you say that I am?" is that the different answers begin with different assumptions about what divinity is. If we were to ask the question, "Must divinity be uncreated?" a person of the Hebrew faith would say yes—but a first- or second-century pagan would say not necessarily.[8] In other words, for a Jewish believer, being eternal and uncreated is part of the very definition of divinity. But in the Greco-Roman pantheon, gods who are not eternal can come into being, often as the result of the procreation of older gods. Thus when we examine some of the alternative views of Christ, he can be both divine and created in the sense that he is the "child" of a pair of deities who "gave birth" to his existence.

---

[8]I use the word *pagan* to describe the traditional/civic religion of the Greco-Roman pantheon.

On the other hand, if we were to ask whether there could be degrees of divinity, the Hebrew would say no, but the pagan would say yes.[9] For the Jewish believer, a being is either divine or not; there can be no degrees. If a being is created, that being is not divine. If a being is uncreated, that being is divine, and there is only one of those: God. Therefore, for some of the early views of Christ, the fact that he is a mediator between God and humanity means that he cannot be divine because divinity is a status reserved for the Father alone. But for the pagan believer, there is a hierarchy of divinity, sometimes even including the top of the human social ladder, royalty. The point is that for two of the five views of Christ, he can be "quasi-divine," that is, less divine than the highest god(s) but more divine than the lowest ones.

If we were to ask, must divinity be immutable and impassible? the Jewish believer would say that these attributes are also part of the very definition of divinity; that is, divinity is unchanging, and divinity cannot suffer. But a pagan would probably agree with the Jews on this one. Apart from the idea that a god can come into being from nonexistence (which is, after all, a form of change), many pagans would have agreed that a divine being cannot suffer, and so the combination of a human Christ who suffers and dies with a divine Christ who works miracles and teaches truths is a contradiction that is very difficult to overcome. As St. Paul said, "Christ crucified" is "a stumbling block to Jews and foolishness to Gentiles" (1 Cor 1:23). As we will see, the alternative views of Jesus Christ emerged in part to protect the immutability and impassibility of the divine against beliefs in a suffering deity.

THE FIVE VIEWS

The chart at the end of this book titled "Christology Continuum" shows the five views of Christ in the postapostolic age. On one side you will see two forms of adoptionism, Spirit Adoptionism (Christ as prophet) and Angel Adoptionism (Christ as angel).[10] Both of these

---

[9]Talbert, *Development of Christology*, 7-8.

[10]Adoptionism refers to the belief that Jesus was in essence a mere human who was adopted as the Son of God but was not the Son of God by nature. For a general definition of adoptionism, see Papandrea, *Trinity 101*, 73-77; and Papandrea, *Reading the Early Church Fathers*, 77-82, 141-44.

emphasized the humanity of Christ and diminished or denied his divinity. In other words, they protected the immutability and impassibility of the divine by denying that Jesus is divine—thus his humanity and his suffering do not encroach on the assumed attributes of divinity: a deity must be unchanging and incapable of suffering.

On the other side you will see two forms of gnosticism, Docetic Gnosticism (Christ as phantom) and Hybrid Gnosticism (Christ as cosmic mind).[11] Both of these emphasized the divinity of Christ and diminished or denied his humanity. In other words, they protect the immutability and impassibility of the divine by denying that Christ was really human— thus his humanity and his suffering were reduced to an illusion.

In the middle is Logos Christology, the view of the mainstream church, reflecting the teaching of the majority of bishops and theologians. This is the christology that will win out over the others in the debates and councils of the early church, but this is because the majority believed that it is the theology that most faithfully reflected the teachings of the apostles. As we will see, Logos Christology did not deny or diminish either the divinity or the humanity of Jesus Christ but maintained that it was possible (though admittedly paradoxical) to believe in a suffering Savior (Is 53).

Therefore, from the start we acknowledge that of the five early views of Christ, one was considered "orthodox," or correct, and four were (eventually) considered heretical, or incorrect. But we also have to acknowledge that it is difficult to speak about "what the heretics believed," since the actual teachings of those who promoted alternative christologies is often only known to us as reported by their opponents. This is not to say that mainstream bishops and theologians were not accurate when they reported the teachings of their enemies. As far as we know, the reports of theologians like Irenaeus of Lyons and Hippolytus are fairly accurate, if not sympathetic. But we can't be sure they

---

[11]Gnosticism refers to the belief that Jesus was in essence a divine spirit who came to bring secret knowledge (*gnōsis* in Greek). For a general definition of docetism and gnosticism, see James L. Papandrea, *Novatian of Rome and the Culmination of Pre-Nicene Orthodoxy*, Princeton Theological Monographs 175 (Eugene, OR: Pickwick, 2011), 2-4; and Papandrea, *Reading the Early Church Fathers*, 58-77. See also the "Messina Definition" (1966) in Lewis, *Introduction to "Gnosticism*," 17.

give us the whole picture, so we have to tread lightly and try not to make too many assumptions or arguments from silence.

In addition, all five christologies developed over time, as each generation of teachers built on the legacies of their own teachers and others who came before them. So just as the mainstream view came to be increasingly clarified over the years, so the alternative christologies also developed, and all did so in dialogue and debate with each other. I have written elsewhere that "heresy forces orthodoxy to define itself."[12] This is certainly true, but it is also true that orthodoxy forced the alternative christologies to define and further clarify themselves as well. Therefore, it must be admitted that the present study can provide an overview of the five christologies but cannot illuminate the individual beliefs of every version of Christianity in the postapostolic age. Although we boil the options down to five, I do not mean to imply that these are neatly distinct pigeonholes. Rather, they are points on a spectrum, and we can probably assume that there was as much diversity of belief within these factions as there was between them. So we are looking at a continuum of belief, and the five views described in the following chapters are at the same time both generalizations and a helpful way to come to understand what different people believed about Jesus Christ.

When it comes to the two forms of gnosticism, we do have some documents that appear to come from the gnostics themselves, and so we are not entirely limited to relying on their enemies to understand their beliefs. The largest collection of gnostic texts is the Nag Hammadi Library, which is available in English translation.[13] This is a very valuable collection of documents, and it includes some of the most famous gnostic texts, such as the Gospel of Thomas and the Gospel of Philip.[14] However, the versions of the documents that we have are late, probably fourth century, and therefore they are not necessarily a faithful representation of anyone's actual beliefs in the second century. In fact, if the fragments

---

[12]Papandrea, *Trinity 101*, 67-68.

[13]James M. Robinson, ed., *The Nag Hammadi Library in English* (1978; repr., San Francisco: HarperSanFrancisco, 1990).

[14]It was well known, even in the postapostolic age, that these documents were not written by Thomas and Philip, respectively, and therefore they were never considered for inclusion in the New Testament canon. See Papandrea, *Reading the Early Church Fathers*, 122-24.

of Plato's *Republic* that were found with these documents are any indi-
cation, we cannot rely on these texts for accuracy of transmission or
translation.[15] Furthermore, the documents of the Nag Hammadi Library
were collected by one group of Christians in the fourth century, and the
beliefs of that group (whatever they were) would determine which documents were preserved and whether they were edited to conform to the
beliefs of the group. Finally, most of the material in these documents is
not about christology per se, and so the christology has to be gleaned
from wherever it pops up—and in fact many of the Nag Hammadi documents are not helpful at all in revealing the christology of the group that
may be responsible for the document. Most of the gnostic writings tend
to be postresurrection conversations with Christ that are really just a lot
of supposed sayings of Christ strung together.[16] They tell us what they
believed he said but not as much about what they believed he *was*.

All of this has led several scholars to question the very concept of
"gnosticism" in favor of recognizing that there were many forms of
gnosticism. Michael Williams and Karen King want to discontinue
using the term *gnosticism* altogether.[17] But this is counterproductive,
since it would leave us with no alternative but to divide gnosticism
into individual schools, a method that led Irenaeus and Hippolytus to
write their almost unmanageably long treatises on the heresies.[18] I
would argue that it is much more productive to categorize the many
schools of gnosticism by their christology, which leaves us with two
distinct versions of gnostic belief.[19] The third-century theologian Novatian recognized this when he wrote,

---

[15]Lewis, *Introduction to "Gnosticism,"* 8.

[16]J. Zandee, "Gnostic Ideas on the Fall and Salvation," *Numen* 11, no. 1 (1964): 66.

[17]See Lewis, *Introduction to "Gnosticism,"* 18-19.

[18]Irenaeus of Lyons, *Against Heresies*; see Papandrea, *Reading the Early Church Fathers*,
92-97; Hippolytus, *Refutation of All Heresies*; see Papandrea, *Reading the Early Church
Fathers*, 105-11.

[19]I first proposed this way of looking at gnosticism in *Reading the Early Church Fathers*, 58-75.
Both Aloys Grillmeier and Talbert have also proposed similar ways of categorizing christology. Grillmeier saw two kinds of gnosticism evident in the Acts of Peter, one in which Christ
was visible and one in which he was invisible. See Aloys Grillmeier, *Christ in Christian Tradition: From the Apostolic Age to Chalcedon (451)*, trans. John Bowden (Louisville: Westminster
John Knox, 1988), 69. Talbert outlines four christological models, two in which Christ is
preexistent and two in which he is not. See Talbert, *Development of Christology*, 16-17.

And so we do not acknowledge the christ of these heretics, who is said to have existed in appearance but not in reality, for there is nothing real of those things which he has supposedly done, if he himself was a phantom and not real. We do not acknowledge one who has carried in himself nothing of our body, received nothing from Mary, and has not really even come to us, since he appeared without our human nature.

Nor do we acknowledge one who has put on ethereal or other-worldly flesh, as other heretics have supposed, for we could not realize our salvation in him if we could not recognize our solid body in him. Nor do we acknowledge any other christ at all, who carries any other kind of mythical body from the fabrication of heretics.[20]

The first paragraph in the quotation above is directed at docetism and Docetic Gnosticism (Christ as phantom), and the second paragraph is directed at Hybrid Gnosticism (Christ as cosmic mind). Furthermore, I will argue that the two different kinds of gnosticism led to two different lifestyles because their christologies inform their anthropologies (their understanding of what it means to be human) to such an extent that it drove how they behaved and how they treated others.

On the other side of the spectrum, Origen saw two kinds of "Jewish Christianity" (adoptionism).[21] In one, Jesus was a mere human, which is analogous to the category I am calling Spirit Adoptionism (Christ as prophet), and in the other, Jesus, or the spiritual entity that indwelt him, had some kind of preexistence. This is analogous to the category I am calling Angel Adoptionism (Christ as angel).

The heresies, or alternative christologies, come first in the following chapters, not because they came first historically, but because orthodoxy was clarified in response to them. So we will explore the two kinds of adoptionism in the next two chapters, then the two kinds of gnosticism, and then the christology of the mainstream.

Finally, it is important to note at the outset that of the five christologies, four of them will solve the problem of the paradox of a

---

[20]Novatian, *The Rule of Truth (De Trinitate)* 10.6. Translation mine, from James L. Papandrea, *Novatian: On the Trinity, Letters to Cyprian of Carthage, Ethical Treatises; Introduction, Translation, and Notes by James L. Papandrea*, Corpus Christianorum in Translation 22 (Turnhout: Brepols, 2015).

[21]Origen, *Against Celsus* 5.61.

suffering Savior by making a radical separation between Jesus and "the Christ," as if they are two different entities (or in one case, as if the former never really existed). Only the Logos Christology of the mainstream church will affirm the unity of Jesus Christ and, even when speaking of the two natures, will refuse to label the humanity "Jesus" and the divinity "Christ."

2

CHRIST AS ANGEL

Angel Adoptionism

Writing about the Ebionites, Origen said the following: "Let it be admitted, moreover, that there are some who accept Jesus, and who boast on that account of being Christians, and yet would regulate their lives, like the Jewish multitude, in accordance with the Jewish law, and these are the twofold sect of Ebionites, who either acknowledge with us that Jesus was born of a virgin, or deny this, and maintain that He was begotten like other human beings."[1] Many have simply assumed that Origen was mistaken, confusing doctrinally orthodox Jewish Christians for a sect of Ebionites.[2] Others have chalked it up to the fact that eventually the name "Ebionite" came to be an umbrella term for all adoptionists. However, I would like to suggest that perhaps Origen knew what he was talking about. As we examine early christology, there is evidence of two distinct schools of thought within the adoptionist camp. In other words, admitting that the name

---

[1]Origen, *Against Celsus* 5.61. Unless otherwise specified, quotations from the church fathers are taken from the Ante-Nicene Fathers collection.

[2]See, for example, Richard Bauckham, "The Origin of the Ebionites," in *The Image of the Judaeo-Christians in Ancient Jewish and Christian Literature*, ed. Peter J. Tomson and Doris Lambers-Petry (Tubingen: Mohr Siebeck, 2003), 163. However, I tend to agree with Bauckham that the term "Nazarenes" (or "Nazoreans") from Epiphanius, *Panarion* 29, is probably a label that originally referred to Jewish Christians in general, and so the name does not necessarily reflect a heretical sect, though it is confused and contrasted with the Ebionites in the literature. See Bauckham, "Origin of the Ebionites," 162, and n. 2. See also Joseph Verheyden, "Epiphanius on the Ebionites," in Tomson and Lambers-Petry, *Image of the Judaeo-Christians*, 184, 187.

"Ebionite" is indeed a catchall and may not have been embraced by both camps at the time, nevertheless there appear to be two kinds of adoptionists: one that accepted the virgin birth of Jesus Christ and one that did not. This chapter will be dedicated to the former.

As is well known, the name "Ebionite" has the connotation of voluntary poverty. In fact this may be one of the rare cases in which the adherents of a heterodox sect actually got to name themselves. According to Epiphanius, (some) early adoptionists called themselves "Ebionites" (or "poor ones") as a way of identifying with Christ and the early Christians in the book of Acts, who sold their possessions and held everything in common.[3] Epiphanius corrects the erroneous story that the founder of the sect was a man named Ebion, and he uses the term "Ebionite" to mock the "poverty" of their adoptionist christology. However, although Epiphanius is a valuable source for understanding early adoptionism, he himself is a later witness and conflates the two kinds of adoptionism into one sect that rejected the virgin birth. Nevertheless, the evidence suggests that there were some adoptionists who accepted the virgin birth of Christ and perhaps can be considered a minority group within the category of Ebionite.[4] These adoptionists understood Jesus of Nazareth as a mere human but took the spiritual Christ to be a separate entity, specifically an angel.[5] As we will see, by separating the man Jesus from the "angel Christ," these adoptionists

---

[3]Epiphanius, *Panarion* 30.17. See also Bauckham, "Origin of the Ebionites," 177-79. In calling themselves Ebionites, they apparently took Jesus' preaching literally—specifically the Lukan version of the saying, "Blessed are you who are poor (Lk 6:20)." Of course, if we can assume that Angel Adoptionists were content with canonical Matthew, then they would have read, "Blessed are the poor *in spirit*" (Mt 5:3)—and therefore perhaps they should not be called Ebionites; rather the term should be reserved for those adoptionists who edited Matthew, in this case to conform to Luke.

[4]It may be that this group should not be called Ebionite at all and that the term should be reserved for those adoptionists who denied the virgin birth (see the chapter on Spirit Christology, below). However, it would be too speculative to try to identify them with the Nazarenes or another known group. For the purposes of the present study, I will tend to prefer the term "adoptionist," though the term "Ebionite" is used synonymously.

[5]In the same way that some gnostics separated the spiritual Christ from the earthly "man" Jesus, in what Birger Pearson calls a "separation christology," some adoptionists also found it convenient to separate the mere human Jesus from "the Christ." See Birger A. Pearson, *Ancient Gnosticism: Traditions and Literature* (Minneapolis: Fortress, 2007), 37-38. The difference, of course, is that in the adoptionist version of "separation christology," no divinity is ascribed to the spiritual entity; rather it is a created being, an angel.

were able to account for the miraculous nature of Jesus' ministry while still holding to an essentially Jewish understanding of Christ as a mere human—possibly anointed by God but indwelt by an angel. This is one of the early explanations of Christ that has been called angel christology, and specifically what I am calling Angel Adoptionism.

Before going further, it must be clarified that I am not talking about what is sometimes called *angelomorphic* christology. This term usually refers to the early Christian belief that the appearances of the "Angel of the Lord" in the Old Testament are in reality appearances of the pre-incarnate Logos.[6] This is, in fact, a common element in the Logos Christology of the apologists and early theologians and will be addressed in chapter six below. While descriptions of the so-called angelomorphic christology acknowledge that certain conceptions of Christ may have been influenced by Jewish speculation on angelic mediators, nevertheless the "Angel" in this case is a reference to the Son's relationship to the Father as messenger to sender and is not meant to be understood as a created being.[7] The Angel of the Lord is still the divine Logos. In what I am calling Angel Adoptionism, however, the angel in question is neither divine nor eternal. It is possible that some adherents of Angel Adoptionism did believe that their Christ was also the Angel of the Lord in the Old Testament; however, this does not seem to be the norm, and in any case, their understanding of the separation of the Christ/angel from the man Jesus, as well as their belief that the indwelling spiritual entity was a created being, sets them apart from the christology of the apologists and early theologians.

THE CHRISTOLOGY OF ANGEL ADOPTIONISM

Angel Adoptionism assumes that a mere human, known as Jesus of Nazareth, was justified in the eyes of God by his perfect obedience to

---

[6]Based on the conviction that "no one can see God and live" (Ex 33:20; 1 Tim 6:16), the early apologists and theologians reconciled the obvious fact that Jesus Christ was visible by reading these passages as "no one can see God *the Father* and live," and therefore anyone who saw God in the Old Testament was actually seeing God the Son, the preexistent and preincarnate divine nature of Jesus Christ. See James L. Papandrea, *Novatian of Rome and the Culmination of Pre-Nicene Orthodoxy* (Eugene, OR: Pickwick, 2011), 7-8, 30-31, 42-43, 97, 102-3.

[7]See Bogdan G. Bucur, "The Angelic Spirit in Early Christianity: Justin, the Martyr and Philosopher," *Journal of Religion* 88, no. 2 (2008): 190-208. Bueur applies the term to pneumatology.

the law. As a reward, he was adopted as a son of God and given the gift of an indwelling of an angelic spirit, who is called Christ, but who is not divine and is usually not thought to be preexistent. However, while most adoptionists would say that the indwelling took place at Jesus' baptism, Angel Adoptionists apparently believed that the indwelling took place proactively at his conception, the result of divine foreknowledge. Thus they could accept the mainstream Christian doctrine of the virgin birth without ascribing divinity to the person of Jesus. Most Angel Adoptionists probably believed that the Christ angel was created at the time of Jesus' conception. The union of man and angel begins at conception, but this union is temporary since the indwelling angel was believed to have left Jesus alone on the cross.

Note that in Angel Adoptionism it is not the case that Jesus *is* an angel, but rather that he was indwelt by an angel.[8] Jesus is a mere human, virgin birth notwithstanding, and thus his divinity is denied.[9] Therefore, in describing Angel Adoptionism, it would be accurate to say that Christ is an angel, but not that *Jesus* is an angel.[10] This separation of Jesus from the Christ/angel is a hallmark of adoptionism (as it is also a hallmark of gnosticism).[11]

---

[8]Tertullian, *On the Flesh of Christ* 14. In the first part of chapter 14, Tertullian is refuting some view that Christ came as an angel. However, almost as an aside toward the end of the chapter, he contrasts this with the christology of "Ebion," who said that Jesus was a mere man and that "there was an angel in him." It seems there were those in the early church who speculated that Jesus was an archangel; however, this would be more akin to gnosticism, since it denied the humanity of Jesus, as Epiphanius states in *Panarion* 30.14.5-6. Note that Epiphanius accuses the Ebionites of "trickery," showing themselves "in many forms." He sees the contradiction but does not realize that those who deny the humanity of Jesus are not really adoptionists— though they may be some kind of Jewish docetics. In *Panarion* 30.3.3, Epiphanius also mentions some Ebionites who seem to describe Christ in gnostic terms, and it may be that either Epiphanius was confusing some earlier docetic/gnostic sects with the Ebionites or that by Epiphanius's time there was a syncretism of christologies that created an Ebionite/gnostic hybrid. In any case, to the degree that these early gnostics diminished the humanity of Jesus, they probably divinized (and worshiped) the spiritual entity of the Christ/angel, and so they would fall more naturally under one of the docetic/gnostic categories. See J. G. Davies, "The Origins of Docetism," *Studia Patristica* 6 (1962): 15-17. See also Brian McNeil, "The Quotation at John XII 34," *Novum Testamentum* 19, no. 1 (1977): 22-33; John W. Marshall, "The Objects of Ignatius' Wrath and Jewish Angelic Mediators," *Journal of Ecclesiastical History* 56, no. 1 (2005): 3-4, 17; and Verheyden, "Epiphanius on the Ebionites," 193-94.

[9]Tertullian, *On the Flesh of Christ* 14.

[10]Epiphanius, *Panarion* 30.16.4.

[11]See Epiphanius, *Panarion* 30.14.4. Epiphanius explains the separation of Jesus (the human) from the Christ (who "entered him").

Therefore, not only is there an ontological difference between the Father and the Son (Jesus), there is an ontological difference between the Father and the indwelling Christ/angel (who is on the creaturely side of the Creator/created divide) and between the indwelling Christ/angel and the man Jesus. Thus the Christ/angel is neither divine nor human but is created, either at the time of Jesus' conception or (for some) at some point in preexistent time.[12] The union of Jesus and the Christ/angel is not a union of the human and the divine nor is it an incarnation; it is primarily an indwelling and an empowerment of a mere human, and even then only temporarily: from conception to crucifixion. After his death, Jesus was not raised, and we can safely assume that references to his resurrection were taken as nothing more than a metaphor for eternal life.

According to Irenaeus, the Ebionites only used the Gospel of Matthew, though he does not say (as others do) that they had edited the Gospel.[13] Is Irenaeus mistaken—has he forgotten to mention that the Gospel of Matthew had been edited to remove the birth narrative? Or does he know of some adoptionists who used canonical Matthew? While he does not distinguish between two different kinds of Ebionites as Origen would later do, it is entirely possible that Angel Adoptionists were content to use canonical Matthew (since they accepted the virgin birth) while the majority of the Ebionites (Spirit Adoptionists) used an edited version of Matthew (the so-called Gospel of the Ebionites?) with the birth narrative removed to conform with their rejection of the virgin birth.

Several scholars have recognized that the letter to the Hebrews in the New Testament contains elements that seem to be a refutation of

---

[12]Epiphanius, *Panarion* 30.16.2. Epiphanius explains that these adoptionists believed the Christ entity came in the form of a dove at Jesus' baptism, but that Christ was "created like one of the archangels."

[13]Irenaeus of Lyons, *Against Heresies* 1.26.2. Note that Irenaeus says that the Ebionites' "opinions with respect to the Lord are similar to those of Cerinthus and Carpocrates." This seems strange, given that these two teachers were gnostics—the christological opposite of adoptionism—until we recognize that Cerinthus and Carpocrates belonged to the category of Hybrid Gnosticism, which also separated Jesus from "the Christ" in a way that reduced the incarnation to a kind of indwelling (see chap. 4). For a discussion of the various Ebionite gospels, see chap. 3.

some form of angel christology.[14] However, there is significant disagreement over whether the angel christology in question is a form of adoptionism or a form of (Hybrid) Gnosticism. In any case, the author of Hebrews does affirm that Christ is superior to the angels, which seems to imply that the targeted heresy reduced Christ to the status of a created angel (Heb 1:4-14). The assumption for the author of Hebrews is that if *Christ* is to be the Savior of humanity, he must become human, not simply indwell a man or be disguised as a human.

THE MAJOR PROPONENTS AND THEIR PRIMARY DOCUMENTS

The earliest known version of Angel Adoptionism may be the sect known as the Elkasaites, or as Epiphanius calls them, the Sampsaeans.[15] They were said to be founded by a man named Elxai, who came from a Jewish-Christian sect called the Ossaeans around the turn of the second century.[16] The Elkasaites were adoptionists who followed (to varying degrees) the Jewish laws but who believed that Christ was a created spiritual being who entered into a human form (the body of Adam) from time to time throughout history.[17] They said that the Holy Spirit is Christ's sister, and both are described as being ninety-six miles tall, which as we will see is an interesting parallel to a description in Hermas's *The Shepherd*.

The eighth book of the Sibylline Oracles portrays the Christ as one who first appeared as the angel Gabriel and then, after the annunciation to Mary, breathed himself into her to be born as a human.[18] Here the virgin birth is affirmed, but the one born is the same as the angel Gabriel.

---

[14]See, for example, Marshall, "Objects of Ignatius' Wrath," 13; McNeil, "Quotation at John XII 34," 27-28; and Michael Goulder, "Hebrews and the Ebionites," *New Testament Studies* 49 (2003): 393-406.

[15]Epiphanius, *Panarion* 53. Hippolytus also mentioned Elkasaites in *Refutation of All Heresies* 9.8-12.

[16]Epiphanius, *Panarion* 19. Epiphanius says this happened during the reign of Trajan (98–117 CE).

[17]Epiphanius, *Panarion* 53.1.8. See also Hippolytus, *Refutation of All Heresies* 9.9. Here Hippolytus relates that for the Elkasaites, the birth of Jesus was neither the first nor the last time that Christ took on a human body and appeared on earth. He is a being whose soul is described as being "transferred from body to body." However, Hippolytus seems to be saying that they also denied the virgin birth, though he could of course be conflating them with other adoptionists.

[18]Marshall, "Objects of Ignatius' Wrath," 16.

He is described as an "eternal creature."[19] Similarly, the Testament of Dan describes a savior-mediator who is an angel or archangel.[20]

The most prominent example of Angel Adoptionism from the early Church would have to be the document known as *The Shepherd* of Hermas.[21] In *The Shepherd*, the savior is an angel called the "angel of justification," who seems to be identified with the archangel Michael. Although the angel is often understood to be Jesus, he is never named as Jesus, and so it is more accurate to say that this angel is Christ— the spiritual entity who indwelt Jesus.[22] As the Elkasaites had done, the angel is described as being supernaturally tall.[23]

The adoptionism of Hermas can be seen in the fact that the reward for right living is a "partnership" with the Holy Spirit, who is described as Creator.[24] The Holy Spirit is called the Son of God and is also described as divine, preexistent, and the spirit of prophecy.[25] The Son of God (the Holy Spirit) is said to be the law, while the "great and glorious angel," who is distinct from the Son of God, is the one who puts the law into the hearts of believers.[26] Therefore the Holy Spirit is not the same as the angel of justification. It seems, rather, that the Son of God is the Holy Spirit, who may indwell believers and inspire prophecy, but the spiritual entity who indwelt Jesus was a mediator angel (Michael) who is called the angel of justification. Thus divinity

---

[19]Sibylline Oracles 8.449-90.

[20]Testament of Dan 6.

[21]See James L. Papandrea, *Reading the Early Church Fathers: From the Didache to Nicaea* (Mahwah, NJ: Paulist Press, 2012), 30-32. Note that in the allegory, the Shepherd is not Christ but is the messenger who brings the vision to Hermas, much like the angel messenger in the book of Revelation. Many authors have situated *The Shepherd* within the camp of angel christology, though some define that in the docetic sense. For example, see McNeil, "Quotation at John XII 34," 27. Note that there is a wide diversity of interpretations among scholars, including disagreement over whether the document in its present form is the product of one author. According to the tradition, it was written by Hermas, who is supposed to be the brother of Bishop Pius I of Rome, placing the document in the mid-second century.

[22]Marshall, "Objects of Ignatius' Wrath," 14.

[23]Hermas, *The Shepherd* 67.2 (Parable 8.2); 83.1 (Parable 9.6). Cf. Epiphanius, *Panarion* 53.

[24]Hermas, *The Shepherd* 59.5-7 (Parable 5.6). See also 55.7 (Parable 5.2) and 69.5 (Parable 8.3). See also Aloys Grillmeier, *Christ in Christian Tradition: From the Apostolic Age to Chalcedon (451)* (New York: Oxford University Press, 2004), 54-55, 78.

[25]Hermas, *The Shepherd* 43.9 (Commandment 11), 59.5 (Parable 5.6), 78.1 (Parable 9.1), 89.2 (Parable 9.12).

[26]Hermas, *The Shepherd* 69.2-3 (Parable 8.3).

and preexistence are reserved for the Father and his Holy Spirit. The Holy Spirit, although described as the Son, may be little more than an extension of the Father, personified in the Father's law. But the point is that Jesus Christ is entirely created, being the product of Jesus the "man of flesh" indwelt by the Christ, who is the mediating angel of justification.[27]

The only named teacher of this form of adoptionism is Lucian of Antioch (ca. 240–312 CE). Often described as a precursor to (and sometimes a teacher of) Arius, he was apparently an adoptionist who accepted the virgin birth of Jesus but who taught that the Christ (the Logos) was a created being. Apart from that, we know very little about him, and what has been written about him is often unreliable. It is said, however, that St. Helena, the mother of the emperor Constantine, was a student of Lucian, and this connection—if true—could be thought to explain the emperor's own "Eusebian" leanings (before the Council of Nicaea), not to mention those of his son Constantius.[28]

SUMMARY AND IMPLICATIONS

While the majority of Ebionites rejected the virgin birth of Jesus, some adoptionists apparently accepted it, which may have made them seem more acceptable to mainstream Christianity and which meant that they did not need to write (or edit) their own gospels. They seem to have been content with canonical Matthew. Their christology envisioned a savior who was the product of a miraculous conception in which a created angel (or archangel, variously identified

---

[27]J. N. D. Kelly, *Early Christian Doctrines*, rev. ed. (San Francisco: Harper & Row, 1978), 94. Kelly saw in *The Shepherd* "three distinct personages": the Father, the Son/Holy Spirit, and Jesus Christ. He clarifies that before the incarnation, there were only two, the Father and the Son/Holy Spirit, since Jesus Christ is entirely created and is elevated to partnership with the divine as an adoptionist reward for obedience to the law. Kelly calls Hermas's christology "an amalgam of binitarianism and adoptionism, though it made an attempt to conform to the triadic formula accepted in the Church."

[28]The myth that Constantine forced his own theology on the Council of Nicaea is easily disproved when one notices that before the council, the emperor seems to be leaning toward Arianism, as evidenced by his correspondence leading up to the council. In any case, in his letters to Alexander and Arius, Constantine demonstrated that he did not understand the importance or the nuances of the theological debate and downplayed that issue in favor of what he saw as the more important debate over the date of Easter.

with Gabriel or Michael) indwelt a mere human. This assumes that a distinction is made between the indwelling angel (Christ) and the man (Jesus) as two separate entities. However, neither Christ nor Jesus is divine—both are created, though the Christ may be considered to have been created in advance of the conception of Jesus. This is not an incarnation, but rather a possession—different from demon possession only because of the benevolence of the indwelling spiritual presence.

This christology is adoptionist because the indwelling is taken to be a reward for obedience to the law, although realized retroactively by divine foreknowledge. Furthermore, the soteriology associated with this christology seems to be based on merit for human effort. That being the case, we might ask why this christology would be attractive in the early centuries of the life of the church. The answer probably lies in the fact that in the early church, and especially in the East, there was enough of a remnant of the classical world's anthropological optimism that many Christians were willing to see the Christian life as progress toward virtue with an expectation of righteousness or even perfection. If we think of an intersection of Jewish sensibilities and classical optimism, we can find enough justification for adoptionism in general, and with Angel Adoptionism specifically, it had the added "benefit" of safeguarding monotheism by keeping divinity radically separated from the created order. Only the Father (possibly with his Holy Spirit) is divine, while Jesus Christ—both Jesus and Christ—are created and are therefore not divine.[29] This allows for a spiritual indwelling in the man Jesus without the suggestion that the Creator had entered creation.

Unfortunately, we don't know enough about the adherents of Angel Adoptionism to know whether their lifestyle reflected their christology. If it is true that early adoptionists can trace their lineage back to the so-called Judaizers of the Pauline letters, and if it is true that adoptionism was primarily a Jewish-Christian phenomenon, then it would be reasonable to assume that the teachers of this school of

---

[29]McNeil, "Quotation at John XII 34," 27.

thought would advocate closer adherence to the Jewish laws and perhaps even a measure of asceticism. However, we cannot know for sure if the Angel Adoptionists practiced vegetarianism or aquarianism (the use of water instead of wine in the Eucharist) as the other Ebionites seem to have done.

3

CHRIST AS PROPHET

Spirit Adoptionism

Origen called the Ebionites a "twofold sect," and Eusebius followed him in recognizing two factions within the category of
Ebionite.[1] As I have argued, there is sufficient evidence to take them
at their word. The Angel Adoptionists described in the previous
chapter seem to have made up a minority group under the Ebionite
umbrella. On the other hand, most Ebionites were what I am calling
Spirit Adoptionists.[2]

Spirit Adoptionism is not to be confused with some early Logos
Christology in which the apologists sometimes blurred the distinction
between the Holy Spirit and the preincarnate or postascension Christ.[3]
While it is possible that Spirit Adoptionism may have been influenced
by this trend in some of the apologists, this early Logos Christology
(see chapter six) is not adoptionism because even when the second
and third persons of the Trinity are confused, the full divinity of the

---

[1]Origen, *Against Celsus* 5.61. See also Eusebius of Caesarea, *Ecclesiastical History* 3.27.

[2]Philip J. Rosato, "Spirit Christology: Ambiguity and Promise," *Theological Studies* 38, no. 3
(1977): 434.

[3]See James L. Papandrea, *Novatian of Rome and the Culmination of Pre-Nicene Orthodoxy*
(Eugene, OR: Pickwick, 2011), 1-15. These early attempts to explain the Trinity are sometimes
referred to as "binitarian"; however, this term is often unhelpful because it does not distinguish between the "binitarianism" of early Logos Christology and that of the adoptionists.
Nevertheless, see Larry W. Hurtado, *Lord Jesus Christ: Devotion to Jesus in Earliest Christianity* (Grand Rapids: Eerdmans, 2003).

second person is affirmed, and no distinction is made between Jesus and "the Christ."[4]

Both forms of adoptionism made this distinction and denied the divinity of Jesus Christ. But whereas the Angel Adoptionists also denied the divinity of the indwelling entity (the Christ is a created angel), Spirit Adoptionism may have allowed for the divinity of the anointing entity, since "the Christ" was for them equivalent to the Holy Spirit.[5] Therefore the name *Spirit* Adoptionism refers to the belief that it was the Holy Spirit who empowered the man Jesus, much like the prophets of the Old Testament. He was inspired by the Holy Spirit but was only a recipient of the Holy Spirit, not a giver of the Holy Spirit, as the mainstream church would affirm (see, e.g., Jn 20:22).

THE CHRISTOLOGY OF SPIRIT ADOPTIONISM

Irenaeus described the Ebionites in general, and we should assume that his description is fairly accurate for the majority of the Ebionites, the Spirit Adoptionists.[6] According to Irenaeus (and unlike their Angel Adoptionist counterparts), they rejected the accounts of the miraculous birth of Jesus, believing him to be the biological son of Joseph.[7] Like all adoptionists, they believed Jesus was a mere human who transcended the rest of humanity by excelling in righteousness. As a reward for his moral progress and perfect fulfillment of the law, he was adopted by God at his baptism. After Jesus was baptized (not at his conception, as the Angel Adoptionists believed), the Christ Spirit descended on him in the form of a dove and entered into him.

---

[4]Irenaeus of Lyons, *Against Heresies* 3.9.3; 3.11.7. See Bogdan G. Bucur, "The Angelic Spirit in Early Christianity: Justin, the Martyr and Philosopher," *Journal of Religion* 88, no. 2 (2008): 193. See also Aloys Grillmeier, *Christ in Christian Tradition: From the Apostolic Age to Chalcedon (451)* (New York: Oxford University Press, 2004), 198; and Anthony Briggman, "Spirit-Christology in Irenaeus: A Closer Look," *Vigiliae Christianae* 66 (2012): 1-19.

[5]In the Gospel of the Hebrews, the Holy Spirit is described as the Savior's mother. Quoted in Origen, *Commentary on John* 1.12.87 (on John 1:3). On the other hand, Spirit Adoptionists could just as easily have believed that the Holy Spirit was a created entity.

[6]Irenaeus of Lyons, *Against Heresies* 3.21.1; 5.1.3.

[7]See also Tertullian, *On the Flesh of Christ* 14; *Prescription Against Heretics* 33.11; Eusebius of Caesarea, *Ecclesiastical History* 3.27; and Epiphanius, *Panarion* 30.20, 30-31. See also Rosato, "Spirit Christology," 434; and Joseph Verheyden, "Epiphanius on the Ebionites," in *The Image of the Judaeo-Christians in Ancient Jewish and Christian Literature*, ed. Peter J. Tomson and Doris Lambers-Petry (Tubingen: Mohr Siebeck, 2003), 200-201.

Thus for them the Christ Spirit is one and the same with the Holy Spirit, who anoints and fills the mere human Jesus.[8]

According to the Spirit Adoptionists, after his baptism Jesus was given power from God through the Holy Spirit and was therefore able to perform miracles.[9] They also believed that the Christ (the Holy Spirit) withdrew from Jesus before his death on the cross. Some apparently reasoned that the Holy Spirit could not participate in the passion because he is divine and therefore impassible. Jesus' cry of dereliction from the cross ("My God, my God, why have you forsaken me?") would have been taken as the moment at which the Holy Spirit left him. And although the Spirit Adoptionists may have believed in a future general resurrection, most apparently did not believe that Jesus rose from the dead.[10] More likely, they understood resurrection as a metaphor for eternal life, and any reports of postresurrection appearances would have been taken as a spiritual visitation, not as a bodily resurrection.

As Epiphanius described their belief, "the Spirit—that is, the Christ—came to him and put on the man called Jesus."[11] Therefore, it could be said that Jesus *became* Christ at his baptism, but he ceased to be Christ at the cross.[12] So the empowering spiritual entity (the Holy Spirit) may have been considered divine by some adoptionists, but the anointing is temporary and is not a union that could be considered an indwelling (let alone an incarnation), but rather an

---

[8]Epiphanius, *Panarion* 28.1.5; 30.14.4; 30.16.3. See Verheyden, "Epiphanius on the Ebionites," 193.

[9]The name "dynamic monarchianism" is a reference to the power (*dynamis* in Greek) granted to Jesus by God. In this way the oneness (monarchy) of God is demonstrated by the belief that Jesus was a mere human and therefore not divine. Any power he has comes from the one God, who is the Father.

[10]Rosato, "Spirit Christology," 433. Their belief in resurrection in general was probably similar to that of the Pharisees, who believed in resurrection in general but denied the resurrection of Jesus (see Acts 23:8). On the other hand, Jerome knows of a passage in the so-called Gospel of the Hebrews in which Jesus appears to James the Just after the resurrection. Jerome, *Illustrious Men* 2.

[11]Epiphanius, *Panarion* 30.3.6, in *The Panarion of Epiphanius*, book 1, trans. Frank Williams (Leiden: Brill, 1987).

[12]Verheyden, "Epiphanius on the Ebionites," 198. The language of "becoming" may not be very helpful here, since it could be confused with a doctrine of incarnation. However, the Ebionite Christ is not the result of incarnation but rather anointing (Spirit Adoptionism) or indwelling (Angel Adoptionism).

inspiration or empowerment. This makes Jesus a prophet, anointed and inspired by (or filled with) the Holy Spirit, but no more so than the prophets of the Old Testament. Indeed, this is exactly what we should expect if the early church fathers were correct in their assumption that adoptionism is the legacy of Paul's "Judaizers."[13]

In Spirit Adoptionism, Jesus is not preexistent. The "Christ-Spirit" may be said to be preexistent because he is the Holy Spirit. But Spirit Adoptionism is not a christology of the incarnation of a preexistent divinity; it is the anointing of a mere human by the Holy Spirit, who may be divine or may also have been created, according to some Spirit Adoptionists. The union of human and divine in "Jesus Christ" is the anointing of the man Jesus by the Christ (the Holy Spirit), an anointing that was temporary, from Jesus' baptism to his crucifixion. What is more, this anointing was the same as that experienced by the prophets and remains available to anyone. Indeed, the Ebionites considered themselves christs in the making and believed that by following the example of Jesus, anyone could become a christ as he did.[14] Jesus was simply "filled with the Spirit" as anyone might be (see 1 Cor 6:19). He was not the first to be anointed, nor was he the last, since the apostles were anointed after him in the same way he was. Thus he is not unique among humanity except by the degree to which he excelled. As with all forms of adoptionism, he is the Savior by example, not by atonement.

THE MAJOR PROPONENTS AND THEIR PRIMARY DOCUMENTS

The earliest teachers of Spirit Adoptionism that we know of are two men called Theodotus. Hippolytus tells us that Theodotus the Elder (also known as Theodotus the Tanner, or Theodotus the Cobbler) taught that Jesus was at one time a sinner, but repented and then progressed in virtue to the point of his baptism, when he received the Christ, who came in the form of a dove and brought him the power to perform miracles.[15] Victor of Rome, who was bishop of that city in

---

[13]Ignatius of Antioch, *Letter to the Magnesians* 8-10; *Letter to the Philadelphians* 6-9.
[14]Hippolytus, *Refutation of All Heresies* 7.22, 34. See also Grillmeier, *From the Apostolic Age to Chalcedon*, 216.
[15]Hippolytus, *Refutation of All Heresies* 7.23.

the last decade of the second century, excommunicated Theodotus the Elder.[16] Theodotus the Younger (also known as Theodotus the Banker) carried on the teaching, emphasizing the distinction between Jesus and the Christ by pointing to Jesus' baptism as the point at which the Christ descended on him.[17] In other words, before Jesus' baptism, he did not have the Holy Spirit.

A group of disciples of Theodotus the Younger called themselves Melchizedekians, after Melchizedek of Genesis 14 and Hebrews 7. They speculated that while Christ may be the mediator of humanity, Melchizedek is the mediator of the angels, and so they were determined to follow the "higher" mediator, Melchizedek.[18] However, it is not clear whether they believed Melchizedek to be a divine being or an archangel. Some may have equated Melchizedek with the Holy Spirit or even with God the Father.[19]

In the third century, one Beryllus of Bostra taught something very much like the Theodotuses, with the exception that he believed it was the Father who indwelt Jesus. He was eventually confronted by Origen at a council, and according to Eusebius, Origen convinced him to recant his heresy and return to orthodoxy.[20] In spite of Beryllus's recantation, it is said that he specifically denied the preexistence of Christ, and in that sense he may have been a transitional figure to the more famous Paul of Samosata.

Paul was bishop of Antioch from the year 260 until he was deposed as a heretic in 268. However, he refused to leave and eventually had to be removed from Antioch by force in 272 CE. He seems to be the last one to try to ignore the prologue to John and openly deny the preexistence of the Logos. After him, even adoptionists would have to accept John 1, though they interpreted preexistence as foreknowledge (as Beryllus may have done), that is, "preexistence in the mind of God." The practical application of Paul's adoptionism is evident in the fact that he attempted to get his see to discontinue singing hymns in praise

---

[16]Eusebius of Caesarea, *Ecclesiastical History* 5.28.
[17]Hippolytus, *Refutation of All Heresies* 7.24.
[18]Epiphanius, *Panarion* 55. See also Grillmeier, *From the Apostolic Age to Chalcedon*, 78.
[19]Epiphanius, *Panarion* 55.5.2-3; 55.9.11-14.
[20]Eusebius of Caesarea, *Ecclesiastical History* 6.33; Jerome, *Illustrious Men* 60.

of Christ.[21] As we will explore in the concluding chapter, it seems that it was a combination of the Spirit Adoptionism of Paul of Samosata with the Angel Adoptionism of Lucian of Antioch that set the stage for the fourth century's version of adoptionism, Arianism.

If the Angel Adoptionists were content to use canonical Matthew as their primary Gospel, Spirit Adoptionists would not be—at the very least Matthew would need to be edited to remove the account of Jesus' miraculous birth. In fact, ancient sources list at least three different names for gospels used by Ebionites; however, it is not clear whether these names represent three distinct gospels or whether they are three ways that patristic writers refer to the same one or two document(s). Scholars are divided in their conclusions, and the debate continues. Where fragments are quoted in the early Christian sources, there is no consensus on which lines belong with which title.[22]

The so-called Gospel of the Nazarenes (or Nazoreans) is mentioned by Jerome, and his comments are sometimes interpreted as though the Nazarenes were a heretical sect and their gospel another gospel based on, but distinct from, canonical Matthew.[23] However, it is equally possible that by "Nazarenes" he is simply speaking of Jewish Christians and that their gospel is the same as the one he says was the original version of canonical Matthew, written in Hebrew.[24] In fact, many early patristic writers believed that Matthew was first written in Hebrew (for a Jewish-Christian audience) and then later translated into Greek.[25] Furthermore, Epiphanius could not say for

---

[21]Eusebius of Caesarea, *Ecclesiastical History* 7.27-30. See also Malchion, *In the Name of the Synod of Antioch Against Paul of Samosata.*

[22]For more detail on this issue, see Verheyden, "Epiphanius on the Ebionites," 188-89.

[23]Jerome, *Illustrious Men* 3. Cf. Epiphanius of Salamis, *Panarion* 29. Epiphanius calls them "Nazoraeans" to distinguish them from a pre-Christian sect called "Nasaraeans." But Epiphanius could not say for sure whether they were adoptionists (*Panarion* 29.7.6). However, he did know of a tradition that said that the fictional character Ebion came from the sect of the "Nazoraeans" (30.1.1; 30.2.1).

[24]Jerome, *Illustrious Men* 2. Cf. Jerome, *Commentary on Matthew* 2; and Epiphanius, *Panarion* 29.9.4. See also Richard Bauckham, "The Origin of the Ebionites," in Tomson and Lambers-Petry, *Image of the Judaeo-Christians,* 172-73; and Verheyden, "Epiphanius on the Ebionites," 184, 188-89.

[25]Jerome, *Illustrious Men* 2-3. See also Eusebius of Caesarea, *Ecclesiastical History* 3.24, 39; 5.8; 6.25.

sure that the "Nazoreans," as he called them, were adoptionist at all.[26] He says that they used the Gospel of Matthew "in its entirety" (i.e., including the virgin birth narrative).[27] Therefore, it is likely that references to a Gospel of the Nazarenes are not preserving the title of an alternative gospel, but rather refer to a version of canonical Matthew in Hebrew or Aramaic used by Jewish Christians, perhaps with some midrashic glosses.[28]

Likewise, the document known as the Gospel of the Hebrews is most likely just another name for canonical Matthew written in Hebrew.[29] It is clear that the Gospel of the Hebrews is not strictly speaking adoptionist, since Jerome indicates that it included a resurrection appearance of Jesus.[30] This could mean that the Gospel of the Hebrews is essentially the same document as the Gospel of the Nazarenes.[31] In any case, the surviving fragments of these documents do not contain enough christology, specifically, to tell us much about the beliefs of the communities that used them.

While the Spirit Adoptionists may have also used the Gospel of the Hebrews/Nazarenes,[32] their own gospel was the Gospel of the Ebionites.[33] Of course, this also need not be an actual title, but could simply be the way that the early writers referred to it. The Gospel of the Ebionites was primarily based on Matthew but was meant to provide an alternative for the Spirit Adoptionist communities.[34] It is not clear

---

[26]Epiphanius, *Panarion* 29.7.6.

[27]Epiphanius, *Panarion* 29.9.4. Epiphanius does say that he is not sure whether their gospel included the genealogy, but it would seem a stretch to assume that his reference to the genealogy includes the birth narrative.

[28]See Jerome, *Against the Pelagians* 3.2.

[29]Epiphanius, *Panarion* 30.3.7.

[30]Jerome, *Illustrious Men* 2.

[31]See Verheyden, "Epiphanius on the Ebionites," 189 n. 30; and Michael Goulder, "Hebrews and the Ebionites," *New Testament Studies* 49 (2003): 397.

[32]Eusebius of Caesarea, *Ecclesiastical History* 3.27. Eusebius says that they only used the Gospel of the Hebrews; however, he may be mistaken, or he may be assuming that the Gospel of the Hebrews and the Gospel of the Ebionites were the same document.

[33]Epiphanius, *Panarion* 30.13.6. Note how Epiphanius could be making a distinction between the Gospel of the Hebrews and the Gospel of the Ebionites by beginning the section with the words "*But their* gospel" (emphasis mine).

[34]Eusebius of Caesarea, *Ecclesiastical History* 6.17. Note that Eusebius mentions an Ebionite teacher named Symmachus, who was known by "his opposition to the Gospel According to Matthew." See also Epiphanius, *Panarion* 30.13.2.

what language it was originally written in, though the consensus seems to be that it was probably written in Greek.[35] It was an attempt at harmonizing the canonical Gospels while at the same time editing the narrative in favor of an adoptionist christology.[36] It did not include the account of the virgin birth but began with the ministry of John the Baptizer.[37] Among other glosses, in the account of Jesus' baptism, the Gospel of the Ebionites emphasized the adoption of Jesus by adding the words of Psalm 2:7 ("Today I have begotten you") to the words of the heavenly voice ("This is my son, the Beloved, with whom I am well pleased").[38] Thus, by removing the virgin birth and by adding to the account of Jesus' baptism, the Gospel of the Ebionites taught a christology that fit within the scope of Spirit Adoptionism.

In addition to their own version of the gospel and probable use of the apocryphal Acts of the Apostles,[39] the Spirit Adoptionists may also have used (and edited?) some of the pseudo-Clementine documents.[40] Certain sections of these documents may show signs that the authors or redactors understood the Holy Spirit, not the Logos, to be the agent of creation.[41] For example, the late third-century *Clementine Homilies* describes the Holy Spirit as the Father's "hand" or wisdom and as the maker of all things in terms that one would expect should be applied to the Logos.[42] The mid-fourth-century *Clementine Recognitions* also seems to make the Holy Spirit the agent of creation.[43] On the other hand, while the texts do call Jesus a prophet, there are sections that seem so orthodox that it would be unlikely they would have been acceptable to an adoptionist.[44] Therefore we cannot conclude

---

[35]Bauckham, "Origin of the Ebionites," 172-73.

[36]Verheyden, "Epiphanius on the Ebionites," 196-98.

[37]Epiphanius, *Panarion* 30.13.6; 30.14.1. See also Bauckham, "Origin of the Ebionites," 164; and Verheyden, "Epiphanius on the Ebionites," 188-89.

[38]Epiphanius, *Panarion* 30.13.7. See also Bauckham, "Origin of the Ebionites," 164.

[39]Epiphanius, *Panarion* 30.16.6-7. On the Ascent of James, see Bauckham, "Origin of the Ebionites," 164-73.

[40]Epiphanius, *Panarion* 30.15.

[41]This could very well be influenced by the tendency of some early apologists to blur the distinction between the Holy Spirit and the preexistent Logos.

[42]*Clementine Homilies* 11.22; 16.12.

[43]*Clementine Recognitions* 6.7.

[44]For example, see *Clementine Recognitions* 1.45.

too much about the *Clementines* other than that they may have been redacted by Spirit Adoptionists, though it seems that the texts were probably reworked again after that. They may represent a later attempt to reconcile or correct adoptionism. In any case, in their present form they are probably too late and too heavily edited to give us much insight into the beliefs of the Spirit Adoptionists other than perhaps the one concept that the Holy Spirit is the agent of creation. Unfortunately, because the documentary evidence is so fragmentary, we are still left with little more than the witness of the opponents of this type of christology.

SUMMARY AND IMPLICATIONS

Like their Angel Adoptionist counterparts, Spirit Adoptionists understood Jesus of Nazareth to be a mere human who earned adoption as the Son of God. As a reward for excelling in righteousness, he was indwelt by a supernatural entity. For the Angel Adoptionists, that entity was a created angel known to them as the Christ. For the Spirit Adoptionists, that entity was the (probably) divine Holy Spirit, also called the Christ.

Spirit Adoptionism is a christology that begins with a Jesus who is not at all unique among humanity. He is not preexistent and is not the result of a virgin birth, but is the biological child of Joseph and Mary. At his baptism, he was "begotten" by God the Father and anointed, inspired and empowered by the Holy Spirit.[45] At this point he had received the Holy Spirit for the first time in his life, and with the Spirit he received the power to be a prophet—to speak for God and perform miracles. After the anointing with the Holy Spirit, Jesus could be called by the title "Christ," but only in the sense that he was empowered to *become* the Christ. He ceased to be the Christ when the Holy Spirit left him alone on the cross (hence the cry of dereliction, "My God, my God, why have you forsaken me?"; see Ps 22:1-2; Mt 27:46; Mk 15:34). He was not physically raised from the dead.

---

[45]Note that, for Spirit Adoptionists, *begetting* equals adoption and takes place at Jesus' baptism. This is in contrast to Logos Christology, in which *begetting* equals generation, which is a function of the preexistence of the Logos.

Some Spirit Adoptionists probably believed that it was the Holy Spirit who preexisted creation and was the agent of creation. As "monarchians," they were trying to protect the oneness of God, as well as the immutability and impassibility of the divine, by conflating the divine Christ (Logos) with the Holy Spirit and by making Jesus a human only, distinct from the Christ/Logos/Holy Spirit. In other words, because Jesus was born, grew, learned and died, he could not be divine, for divinity is immutable and impassible. The emphasis here is on the humanity of Jesus and his anointing for his ministry as prophet. The fact that he was filled with the Spirit is not emphasized because it was understood to be temporary.

Another way to look at this is that while Angel Adoptionism was a christology that emphasized indwelling, Spirit Adoptionism was a christology that emphasized anointing. Neither accepted what we would call an incarnation, since the concept of incarnation assumes a preexistent divine Logos who acquires a human nature—not a mere human who is anointed by a divine Spirit.

Spirit Adoptionism would have been attractive to Jewish believers for the same reasons that Angel Adoptionism was. An optimism regarding human nature that allowed people to assume they could follow the law, combined with a Jewish understanding of the Messiah, would make this brand of adoptionism acceptable to Jews in the Roman Empire. As a christology that understood Jesus primarily in terms of a prophet, Spirit Adoptionism would be the closest christology to traditional Judaism while still accepting Jesus as Messiah. Thus it could be argued that Spirit Adoptionism would be the most "comfortable" of the christological options for Jewish Christians. Significantly, this christology answered the dilemma of Christian monotheism by removing the man Jesus from the realm of divine (thus allowing him to be mutable and passible), and yet it still allowed for divine intervention in the descent of the Holy Spirit.

It should be no surprise, then, that the lifestyle of Spirit Adoptionists (the majority of Ebionites) included a stricter attention to the Jewish laws than one would find in mainstream Christianity.[46] In fact,

---

[46]Epiphanius, *Panarion* 30.2.1-6; Eusebius of Caesarea, *Ecclesiastical History* 6.17.

they were often accused of being legalistic to the point of having mis-understood grace. And although the apocryphal Acts of the Apostles (such as the Acts of Paul or the Acts of Thomas) were not necessarily written by the Spirit Adoptionists, their emphasis on asceticism probably made them popular reading among the Ebionites.[47] Many, if not most, Ebionites were also vegetarians.[48] Some were ascetics. Finally, they seem to have refrained from the use of wine in their Eucharist (a practice now known as aquarianism), possibly as an act of asceticism, or possibly as a way to reject the mainstream belief that Jesus' blood had atoning significance.[49]

---

[47]However, Epiphanius says that at least some of them rejected asceticism (*Panarion* 30.2.6). But note that Epiphanius says their vegetarianism is based on the fact that meat is the result of procreation, which implies that some may have prized celibacy after all.

[48]Epiphanius, *Panarion* 30.15.3. Cf. *Clementine Homilies* 8.15; 12.6.

[49]Irenaeus of Lyons, *Against Heresies* 5.1.3; Hippolytus, *Refutation of All Heresies* 8.13; Epiphanius, *Panarion* 30.16.1.

4

CHRIST AS PHANTOM

Docetism and Docetic Gnosticism

I n the Gospels, when Jesus walked on the water, we are told that for
a moment the disciples thought he was a ghost (Mt 14:26; Mk
6:49). The Greek word for "ghost" is *phantasm*, or phantom. What the
disciples mistakenly thought about Jesus in that moment of con-
fusion is what the group known as "docetics" actually believed and
taught. They said that Christ was not a human, and in fact had no
body at all, but was a phantom. The terms *docetic* and *docetism* come
from the Greek verb *dokein*, meaning "to seem" or "to appear," the
implication being that Jesus only *seemed* or *appeared* to be human,
but in reality he was not. As a label for Christian heretics, our first
extant use of the word is by Hippolytus in the early third century;
however, he seems to use the concept as though his readers already
know it (implying that he did not coin the term), and he used the
terms broadly to include all gnostics.[1]

However, docetism in its purest form actually came before gnosticism and was part of the evolution of gnosticism. Already in the late
first century we can see an anti-docetic argument in the letter of
1 John. In 1 John 4 the author writes, "This is how you can know the
Spirit of God: every spirit that acknowledges Jesus Christ come in the
flesh belongs to God, and every spirit that does not acknowledge Jesus

---

[1]Hippolytus, *Refutation of All Heresies* 8.3. See also Edwin M. Yamauchi, "The Crucifixion and
Docetic Christology," *Concordia Theological Quarterly* 46 (1982): 5.

does not belong to God. This is the spirit of the antichrist" (1 Jn 4:2-3 NAB). The docetics were those who did not believe Jesus Christ had come in the flesh, and John calls them antichrists for their failure to accept the humanity of Christ. Note also that the author begins that letter by claiming not only that he is an eyewitness to the events of the Gospels but also that he *touched* Jesus (1 Jn 1:1).[2] A bit later, in the early second century, the letters of Ignatius of Antioch continue the anti-docetic arguments, and then in the mid-second century, the *Epistula Apostolorum*, a refutation of gnosticism, follows 1 John in placing an emphasis on touching Jesus.[3] The author affirms that Jesus received a human body from Mary and was indeed touched by the disciples.[4] Peter touches the wounds of Jesus, as Thomas does in the Gospel of John, and Andrew is encouraged to see that Jesus' feet do make footprints.[5]

Historically, the adjective *docetic* has been applied in two ways. The first is the broader definition, as Hippolytus and those like him used it. In this sense, *docetism* means that Jesus Christ only appeared to be *human*, though he might have been tangible. This definition applies to all gnostics, including Hybrid Gnosticism (see the next chapter), for it allows that Jesus may have had a body of some kind even though he was not really human.[6] This is what some have called a "quasi-docetic" christology.[7] However, the hybrid christology came along later as a concession to the all but universal acceptance of the canonical Gospels, which present Jesus as being tangible and eating as well as suffering and dying.[8]

---

[2]J. G. Davies, "The Origins of Docetism," *Studia Patristica* 6 (1962): 18.

[3]*Epistula Apostolorum* 2.

[4]*Epistula Apostolorum* 3.

[5]*Epistula Apostolorum* 11. See John J. Gunther, "Syrian Christian Dualism," *Vigiliae Christianae* 25 (1971): 83, 90-91. On the other hand, the *Epistula Apostolorum* mentions Cerinthus by name, who falls more into the hybrid category, demonstrating that like Irenaeus, the early opponents of gnosticism did not always make the distinction with which I am working here.

[6]Simone Pétrement, *A Separate God: The Origins and Teachings of Gnosticism* (San Francisco: HarperSanFrancisco, 1990), 146 (originally published in French as *le Dieu séparé: les origins de gnosticisme* [Paris: Cerf, 1984]). The term "Hybrid Gnosticism" was coined in James L. Papandrea, *Reading the Early Church Fathers: From the Didache to Nicaea* (Mahwah, NJ: Paulist Press, 2012), 58-77.

[7]Yamauchi, "The Crucifixion and Docetic Christology," 5.

[8]According to Robert Grant, the earliest gnostics were those whom I am including in the

The second, more narrowly defined use of *docetism* is to say that not only was Jesus' *humanity* only apparent but also his *corporeality*. He only appeared to be human, and he only appeared to be tangible.[9] It is this second sense in which I am using the word *docetic* to describe the "purely docetic" christology of Docetic Gnosticism in contrast with the "quasi-docetic" christology of Hybrid Gnosticism. The difference between the hybrid christology and the purely docetic christology is the difference between Christ taking the *form* of humanity versus taking the *appearance* of humanity only. Hybrid Gnosticism believed that Christ took the *form* of a human, which allowed him to *appear* to be a baby and a child, to eat and bump into people, and even appear to suffer on a cross. But the purely docetic Christ is a phantom— he does none of these things. He arrives on earth in the *appearance* of

---

purely docetic category: Menander and Saturninus. Robert M. Grant, "The Earliest Christian Gnosticism," *Church History* 22, no. 2 (1953): 81. Indeed, evidence of "proto-gnosticism" in the New Testament is most likely docetic, without the secret knowledge or complicated cosmology that is indicative of true gnosticism. See Michael Slusser, "Docetism: A Historical Definition," *The Second Century: A Journal of Early Christian Studies* 1, no. 3 (1981): 176. Slusser calls the difference between the two a distinction between a later gnostic "scheme in which the 'technical' details of the manifestation have been worked out, and a more naive docetistic one in which these problems have not been faced." On one level, he may be correct, but calling the truly docetic christology "naive" seems to underestimate the importance of the concepts of immutability, impassibility and incorruptibility, and it minimizes the very real differences over the question of the tangibility of Jesus' body. After all, pure docetism did not go away after the hybrid version came on the scene.

[9]Pétrement includes Basilides in the "purely docetic" category. He contrasts two types of docetism: "that which is attributed to Cerinthus (the distinction of two persons in Jesus Christ)" and "that of Saturnilus and Basilides, who, if one believes Irenaeus, said that Jesus only appeared to have a human nature" (Pétrement, *A Separate God*, 319). While Pétrement made a similar distinction to the one I am making here, he admits that Irenaeus did not make this distinction. Slusser puts Basilides with Cerinthus into the hybrid category, quoting Fortescue, "Those who were not gnostic at all, but distinguished Christ the spiritual Saviour from the normal man Jesus" (Slusser, "Docetism: A Historical Definition," 164-65; quoting Adrian Fortescue, "Docetism," in *Encyclopedia of Religion and Ethics*, ed. J. Hastings [New York, 1912], 4:883). The point is not to argue for or against the inclusion of Basilides (or any other gnostic) in one category or the other (since we would then run the risk of pressing the categories further than their usefulness) but to clarify the two different approaches as alternative explanations of the person of Christ. Slusser's article brings to light a 1961 doctoral dissertation by Peter Weigandt (*Der Doketismus im Urchristentum und in der theologischen Entwicklung des zweiten Jahrhunderts*, 2 vols. [Diss. Heidelberg, 1961]), which defines docetism in the more specific sense used here, connects this definition with Cerdo, Marcion and Saturninus (as I do), and refers to the Acts of John as a purely docetic text. However, Slusser argues for the continued use of the "historical" (broader) definition of docetism.

an adult human, with no concession to the manger or the cross.[10] In both kinds of gnostic christology, the apparent humanity of Jesus is just a disguise.[11] Nevertheless, *docetism*, narrowly defined, is a christology in which Jesus is incorporeal and intangible, and any contact he may have had with the human senses was an illusion.

What I am calling two distinct christologies (hybrid and docetic) have been called "contradictions" within docetism.[12] But we can distinguish between them as two different christologies based on the difference of corporeality versus incorporeality, or form versus appearance. Thus, when it comes to the distinction between "Jesus" and "the Christ," Hybrid Gnosticism recognizes a Jesus who is at least tangible and in some way united to the Christ. For the true docetics, however, Christ (if they called him that) is a deity, with no real earthly component—"Jesus" is an illusion, and therefore his suffering isn't real.[13] Whatever people thought they saw during the ministry of Jesus, it was an apparition. It may have "appeared" to be a man, but it was in fact a pure spirit, a phantom. His "body" was an illusion.[14]

This chapter covers what are historically two movements, docetism proper and Docetic Gnosticism. Docetism proper precedes Docetic Gnosticism and continues on in its pure form even after it has evolved into Docetic Gnosticism in some communities. Docetic Gnosticism is a syncretism that incorporated the typical gnostic emphasis of secret knowledge and elaborate cosmologies with their complicated pantheon of deities. However, the non-gnostic form of docetism survived alongside the gnostic version in the followers of Marcion and others, who apparently did not embrace many of the tenets of gnosticism. Nevertheless, original

---

[10]However, both of these concepts, form and appearance (or likeness), occur in Phil 2:7, and it appears that proponents of both of these christological trajectories could use that passage as a prooftext.

[11]Pétrement, *A Separate God*, 146. See also Slusser, "Docetism: A Historical Definition," 172.

[12]Pétrement, *A Separate God*, 152-53.

[13]Tertullian, *Against Marcion* 3.8; 4.42 (note Tertullian's critique that pure spirit cannot give up itself, demonstrating that a docetic crucifixion defies logic). See also Pétrement, *A Separate God*, 146; and Tim Carter, "Marcion's Christology and Its Possible Influence on Codex Bezae," *Journal of Theological Studies* 61, no. 2 (2010): 560, 568. Cf. Slusser, "Docetism: A Historical Definition," 168, 171.

[14]Carter, "Marcion's Christology," 560.

docetism and Docetic Gnosticism are combined in this chapter because they share a common christology—regardless of the absence or presence of other aspects of gnosticism, all of these taught a distinction between the Christ and Jesus, such that Christ was a phantom and Jesus an illusion.

THE CHRISTOLOGY OF DOCETISM AND DOCETIC GNOSTICISM

In a way, even Docetic Gnosticism separated "Jesus" from "the Christ" in the sense that it made a distinction between (as they saw it) the illusion and the reality, respectively. To them, Jesus was an illusion; Christ was the reality, but an entirely intangible reality. He was pure spirit. However, some, like Marcion (whom we will discuss below), would not have used the title "Christ," since that would imply a connection to the Old Testament and the God of the Jews.

It is common to attribute docetism to an emphasis on Platonic dualism taken to the extreme. In other words, Plato had taught that the spiritual was more real than the material, and some (perhaps following the lead of the Neo-Pythagoreans) took that to mean that the spiritual was good but the material was evil. Therefore docetic christology was an attempt to distance the divine Savior from the material world, apparently believing that the phrase "the Word became flesh" (Jn 1:14) was the same as saying, "the Good became evil."

All of this is true; however, there is a deeper philosophical basis for docetism than simply an extreme dualism. The docetic approach to christology probably came from a desire to preserve the immutability of the divine Christ. In other words, the concept of the incarnation, as it was described by the bishops and theologians of the majority church, was taken to be a kind of ontological change in the essence of the divine Logos, and this was considered unacceptable in that it would contradict the concept of immutability, one of the assumed attributes of divinity. Divinity must be eternal, and early docetics would have reasoned that whatever could not come to an end also could not change, since change implies the possibility of corruptibility and death. For example, the Book of Thomas the Contender declares, "That which changes will decay and perish, and has no hope of life from then on."[15] As we will see in the next chapter, in Hybrid Gnosticism, with its elaborate cosmologies that included pairs of deities who begat other deities, apparently the idea of divine beings having a beginning to their existence was not a problem. However, we do not see this in the purely docetic version of gnosticism. In fact, the change from nonexistence to existence is a form of change, so for Docetic Gnosticism (as for mainstream Christianity), divinity must be eternal, and that requires immutability. Any hint of mutability, passibility or corruptibility would be an irreconcilable contradiction.

Docetics may have argued from 1 Corinthians 15:50 that humanity (flesh and blood) could not be saved.[16] In fact, we can see from the second-century treatises on the resurrection that mainstream Christian apologists such as Justin Martyr and Athenagoras were writing against the pagan philosophical belief in the afterlife as a disembodied existence. The docetics apparently followed the philosophical view that the end goal of the human person was to discard the body and be free of it. Therefore, if the "heavenly" existence was an incorporeal existence, and salvation meant being freed from the "prison of the flesh," they must have reasoned that Christ himself would never take on the form of a human body.

In any case, it is probably true that the docetic explanation of Jesus Christ began with the same practical problem that all Christians had—the problem of explaining the humanity of Christ in light of his divinity (or vice versa). The practical, or observational, problem in turn leads to a theological or philosophical explanation. In the case of docetism, the explanation required the complete denial of Jesus' humanity, including his passion. In fact, docetism assumed the old-world understanding of suffering, that it is the result of divine condemnation (even though this view was rejected by Jesus himself, not to mention the book of Job).[17] So for those who took the docetic

---

[15]The Book of Thomas the Contender (in *The Nag Hammadi Library in English*, ed. James M. Robinson [1978; repr., San Francisco: HarperSanFrancisco, 1990], 202). See also Davies, "Origins of Docetism," 13, 15, 30-31.

[16]See Novatian, *On the Trinity* 10.9.

[17]Pétrement, *A Separate God*, 144, see also 146-47, 151.

approach, any suffering ascribed to Jesus was either denied altogether or attributed to an illusion.

Finally, the two different gnostic christologies can be distinguished by their respective implications for anthropology and lifestyle. Hybrid christology, which posited a "useful," though not human, body of Jesus and a separation of the physical Jesus from the spiritual Christ, apparently led to a compartmentalization of the spiritual life of the believer, aloof from the physical, which allowed its adherents to justify a hedonistic lifestyle. The body could be used for any pleasure, or even abuse, without compromising the spirit or the mind. On the other hand, the primary sources attest that those who held to a purely docetic christology tended to be ascetic.[18] As we will see, they denigrated marriage, advocating celibacy for all believers. For example, both the Book of Thomas the Contender and the Authoritative Teaching refer to sexuality (even within marriage) as "bestiality" because it is a function of the human body.[19] In fact, Docetic Gnosticism takes such a low view of the human body that it saw no value in feeding the hungry or helping the poor.[20]

THE MAJOR PROPONENTS AND THEIR PRIMARY DOCUMENTS

I will begin with a brief survey of documents that may exhibit evidence of Docetic Gnosticism. I say "may" because in the case of the documents of the Nag Hammadi Library, we are sometimes dealing with

---

[18]See James L. Papandrea, *Reading the Early Church Fathers: From the Didache to Nicaea* (Mahwah, NJ: Paulist Press, 2012), 58-77.

[19]Authoritative Teaching (in Robinson, *Nag Hammadi Library*, 306). I have not included the Authoritative Teaching among the docetic documents below because there is no real christology in the document to tell whether it is hybrid or docetic. However, I assume that it is docetic because it is ascetic. See Authoritative Teaching (in Robinson, *Nag Hammadi Library*, 306, 308), where the drinking of wine is prohibited. Also, the document makes a clear distinction between the spiritual soul and the material soul (Authoritative Teaching [in Robinson, *Nag Hammadi Library*, 306]). But see Pétrement, *A Separate God*, 485. Pétrement thinks that the Authoritative Teaching is a Valentinian document because of the mention of the bridal chamber. If he is correct, perhaps it represents a possible Eastern (docetic) form of Valentinian Gnosticism, which may have been taught by Theodotus, Bardesanes, Marcus, Axionicus and/or Julius Cassianus.

[20]Ignatius of Antioch, *Letter to the Smyrnaeans* 6.2. See also Helen Rhee, *Loving the Poor, Saving the Rich: Wealth, Poverty, and Early Christian Formation* (Grand Rapids: Baker Academic, 2012), 173-74.

very few references to christology per se, and where we can find evidence of docetism, it is not always conclusive that it is the pure docetism of Docetic Gnosticism. In other words, the absence of the mention of a tangible body of Jesus does not necessarily mean that the authors of these documents did not believe he had one. In fact, the vast majority of the Nag Hammadi documents reflect the christology of Hybrid Gnosticism. There are several logical reasons for this. First of all, the Nag Hammadi cache is late with regard to the evolution of gnosticism, and so it would make sense that as more time goes by there will naturally be more syncretism and more concession to the mainstream church and its affirmation of the humanity of Christ. By the fourth century, it is likely that the documents that would have survived were the ones closest to the mainstream. In addition, the collection of documents was compiled by monks who were either orthodox or hiding their heterodoxy. So the documents they included in their stash would naturally be those that were closer to the orthodox position and therefore more acceptable. If the monks were orthodox, they may not have felt that these documents were heretical enough to destroy them.[21] On the other hand, if they were heterodox, these documents were, perhaps, those perceived as less dangerous should they be found. Nevertheless, there are a few documents from Nag Hammadi in which the christology appears sufficiently docetic in the narrower sense, and so they will be included here for the reader's consideration.

It appears that there was in the early church a Thomas tradition that tended toward the purely docetic. This would not include the Infancy Gospel of Thomas (with its Jesus who could be bumped into), but there are hints of docetism in the Gospel of Thomas, the Acts of Thomas and possibly the Book of Thomas the Contender, and these documents have enough similarities to cause scholars to speculate that they come from the same school of thought.[22]

---

[21]It is also possible that an orthodox group of monks kept the documents as a "library of heresy," as a source of research for mainstream apologetics, so that these gnostic documents could be refuted. In that case, we could speculate that they were hidden away to prevent them from falling into the hands of Christians who would not know how to distinguish them from approved church teaching.

[22]John D. Turner, introduction to The Book of Thomas the Contender (in Robinson, *Nag Hammadi Library*, 199). It is ironic that some docetics may have considered themselves

According to this Thomas tradition, the apostle Thomas, called Didymus (the twin), was actually the twin brother of Jesus.[23] While this may seem as though it implies a body and perhaps even a birth, the fact that Jesus and Thomas look alike has more to do with the fact that Jesus is Christ in disguise. In the Acts of Thomas, we read that at one point Jesus is mistaken for Thomas because they look alike. However, in the context of the story Jesus has appeared out of nowhere, and so it could be read as though Jesus "took on" the appearance of Thomas when he materialized in the room. Even though Jesus and Thomas are presented as twins, the appearance of Jesus as Thomas's identical twin is still just an appearance. In the Book of Thomas the Contender, Jesus says to Thomas, "Now since *it has been said* that you are my twin and my true companion . . . since *you will be called* my brother. . . ."[24] The point is, the assertion that Jesus is a twin of Thomas does not imply human generation. In fact, it was probably meant to say more about Thomas than about Jesus.[25] It is not that being twins makes Jesus human but that it makes Thomas divine. In fact the message of the Thomas school seems to have been along the lines of a typical kind of gnostic salvation by enlightenment: knowing one's true divine (immutable) self.[26] Jesus says to Thomas, "Examine yourself and learn who you are, in what way you exist."[27] Thus Thomas, as their primary apostle, could have been seen as having realized his own divinity. In any case, I will begin with the documents attributed to this Thomas tradition and then move on to the other anonymous documents before coming to the early teachers whom we know by name.[28]

---

followers of Thomas, since he was the one who touched the wounds of Jesus in the canonical Gospel of John. Perhaps the story of Thomas touching the wounds was included in the fourth Gospel specifically to refute a Thomas tradition that was already going off on a docetic tangent.

[23]The Book of Thomas the Contender (in Robinson, *Nag Hammadi Library*, 201).

[24]Ibid. (emphasis added).

[25]It could also be a remnant of an early version of the Hybrid Gnosticism's tendency to understand the cosmos in terms of pairs of deities. That Thomas could be considered a divine parallel or counterpart to Jesus is not out of the question.

[26]For example, see the Gospel of Thomas 70, 88 (in Robinson, *Nag Hammadi Library*, 134, 136).

[27]The Book of Thomas the Contender (in Robinson, *Nag Hammadi Library*, 201).

[28]We will not be concerned here with dating the documents in question, since that is a study in itself and since we cannot be sure of the original form of the documents found at Nag Hammadi.

The Gospel of Thomas. While there is little in this document that is explicitly christological, there is a general and utter disdain for the flesh and the things of the material world. Jesus is made to say, "Wretched is the body that is dependent upon a body [meaning a husband and wife?], and wretched is the soul that is dependent on these two [a child?]."[29] This seems to denigrate not only marriage but love itself. Later Jesus says, "Whoever does not hate his father and his mother *as I do* cannot become a disciple to me."[30] The point is that the disdain for creation that is inherent in docetic dualism comes out as a rejection of human procreation, including marriage, and as an attitude which says that the true believer will be an ascetic.[31] Therefore, while we cannot say for certain that the Gospel of Thomas demonstrates a purely docetic christology, the asceticism and rejection of physical creation are consistent with docetism.[32] Furthermore, if we can speak of a Thomas tradition including the Acts of Thomas, the picture becomes a bit clearer in favor of a docetic "Thomas" christology with its consequent asceticism.

The Acts of Thomas. In the Acts of Thomas, Christ appears so that he can send Thomas into India. When Thomas refuses to go, Christ sells him as a slave to a merchant traveling to India, and in that way Thomas is forced to go and do the will of Christ. Like many of the apocryphal acts, the apostle's ministry amounts to preaching celibacy, as here marriage is referred to as "filthy intercourse." Thomas also tries to talk people out of wanting to have children, because having children leads to worldly cares, greed and eventually sorrow. The message is that creating life only leads to death, and the text implies that married people cannot be saved.

---

[29]Gospel of Thomas 87 (in Robinson, *Nag Hammadi Library*, 135).

[30]Gospel of Thomas 101 (in Robinson, *Nag Hammadi Library*, 137); emphasis added. However, Jesus also goes on to say, "Whoever does not love his father and his mother as I do cannot become a disciple to me." Assuming this reconstruction of the text is accurate, it is so esoteric as to be contradictory and therefore inconclusive. See also Gospel of Thomas 105, in which Jesus says, "He who knows the father and the mother will be called the son of a harlot."

[31]See Gospel of Thomas 27 (in Robinson, *Nag Hammadi Library*, 129). Here fasting is said to lead to salvation. However, in Gospel of Thomas 14, the reader is told that fasting leads to sin.

[32]The phrase "I appeared to them in flesh" does not mean that Jesus had tangible flesh, only that he appeared to. See Yamauchi, "The Crucifixion and Docetic Christology," 11.

Instead, Thomas advocates a spiritual marriage, "that marriage incorruptible and true."

With regard to christology, demons in the story refer to the incarnation as a deception, in which Christ "deceived us by the form which he had put on, and his poverty and his want; for when we saw him such, we thought him to be a man clothed with flesh." The implication, of course, is that he was not. In the account of the martyrdom of Thomas, we find out that "Jesus Christ" is not the true name of the Savior. His true name cannot be known, but "Jesus Christ" is his name only "for a season."

This brings up another aspect of docetism, which is its affinity with modalism. Modalists conceived of the Trinity, not as one God in three persons, but as one person with three names.[33] In this way modalism, like docetism, denied the humanity of Jesus, since for the modalists, the Son was only one manifestation of the Father, "for a season." True docetism, with its radical distinction between divinity and humanity, comes from a similar philosophical "place" as modalism, that is, the desire to protect the divinity of God by safeguarding God's immutability. However, this "safeguarding" requires the distancing of the divine from humanity. We will explore the affinities between docetism and modalism a bit more in the concluding chapter.

The Acts of John. If the docetic christology in the Thomas tradition was illusive, here it is much more clear. In the Acts of John, Jesus is not only intangible but also sometimes invisible.[34] On the other hand, he can be tangible when he wants to be, and then sometimes his body feels soft and at other times hard.[35] But this does not imply a hybrid christology because his "body" is said to be an "immaterial substance."[36]

---

[33]Papandrea, *Reading the Early Church Fathers*, 139-41. Note that, according to Irenaeus, Simon Magus claimed "that it was himself who appeared among the Jews as the Son, but descended in Samaria as the Father, while he came to other nations in the character of the Holy Spirit" (Irenaeus of Lyons, *Against Heresies* 1.23.1).

[34]Acts of John 88.

[35]Acts of John 89. See also Acts of John 90, in which Jesus tugs on John's beard and it hurts for thirty days.

[36]Acts of John 93, 107. To modern ears "immaterial substance" might sound like an oxymoron; however, it would have been assumed that anything that was real had "substance," in the sense of an ontology, even if it was incorporeal. The important word here is "immaterial." See Slusser, "Docetism: A Historical Definition," 167.

Here the tangibility itself is an illusion—he is not tangible by nature; he is immaterial, incorporeal. Sometimes he appears small, at other times very large.[37] He is described as "not having any shape."[38] His eyes never blink.[39] When he walks he leaves no footprints.[40] Apparently the transfiguration is held up as normative for how Jesus was always perceived.[41]

Jesus is further described as a "cross of light" and is also called, among other things, the Word, Jesus, Christ, Father, Son, and Spirit.[42] Here again we see the affinity with modalism in that the divine Christ is not distinct from the Father or the Holy Spirit. Of course if all of this is the case, then he could not suffer.[43] In the Acts of John Christ described his crucifixion as "contrived."[44] He says he was not the one on the cross, implying that there was a vision of a person on the cross that people could see, but he was elsewhere.[45] Jesus explains, "I was reckoned to be that which I am not" (i.e., human).[46] He "became a man apart from this body," but in case anyone should think that using the word "man" means he became human, it is later clarified that he was not a man.[47] The point is that he has no body. Christ further distinguishes himself from humanity and human nature by implying that the goal of the human person is to leave his or her humanity behind and become what Jesus is (i.e., no longer human).[48]

With regard to asceticism, the Acts of John assumes that celibacy is the true calling of all believers and portrays women as tempters of men, obstacles to living the spiritual life. Sex, even within marriage, is called "that foulness."[49]

---

[37] Acts of John 89-90.

[38] Acts of John 98.

[39] Acts of John 89.

[40] Acts of John 93.

[41] Acts of John 90.

[42] Acts of John 98.

[43] Acts of John 101. True to the esoteric nature of these documents, Jesus at one point says that he did not suffer, but then later says he did. It is clear, however, that the crucifixion was an illusion, a vision, in which no real suffering took place.

[44] Acts of John 97-99, 102.

[45] Yamauchi, "The Crucifixion and Docetic Christology," 8-9.

[46] Acts of John 99.

[47] Acts of John 102, 104.

[48] Acts of John 100-101.

[49] Ibid., 63-64, 113.

The Acts of Andrew. We can extrapolate the christology from the Acts of Andrew by looking at what the document says about the goal of the spiritual life. Assuming that the goal is to become like Christ, the way the text describes the perfected person should tell us something about how the author understood the person of Christ. In the Acts of Andrew, the enlightened person is described as "immaterial, holy light, akin to him that is unborn . . . translucent, pure, above the flesh." As the spiritual person approaches likeness to the unborn one (Christ), the person becomes more like him, that is, incorporeal. It appears that it was believed that the more one approaches the likeness of Christ, the closer one comes to immateriality, moving from matter to light. In addition, this document advocates celibacy, calling marriage a "foul and polluted way of life."

The Concept of Our Great Power. In this document, we are told that the Logos first appeared in the east.[50] This seems consistent with the Marcionite claim that Jesus appeared on the earth as an adult in about 30 CE (see under Marcion below). After Judas's betrayal, we are told that the "ruler of hades" was frustrated in his plans to capture Jesus because "the nature of his flesh could not be seized."[51] The use of the word "flesh" here does not imply that he had a body; on the contrary, it was the "nature" of his "flesh" that it was intangible. No one could lay their hands on him.

The Sophia of Jesus Christ. Like the Gospel of Thomas, this is a "postresurrection" dialogue and was possibly influenced by Sethian Gnosticism.[52] The reader is told, "The Savior appeared, not in his previous [preresurrection] form [i.e., visible], but in the invisible spirit. And his likeness resembles a great angel of light. But his resemblance I must not describe. No mortal flesh could endure it, but only pure and perfect flesh, like that which he taught us about

---

[50]The Concept of Our Great Power 44 (in Robinson, *Nag Hammadi Library*, 315).

[51]The Concept of Our Great Power 42 (in Robinson, *Nag Hammadi Library*, 314).

[52]Douglas M. Parrott, introduction to Eugnostos the Blessed and The Sophia of Jesus Christ (in Robinson, *Nag Hammadi Library*, 220-21). Note that we are told the Savior laughs (The Sophia of Jesus Christ [in Robinson, *Nag Hammadi Library*, 222]).

on the mountain."[53] Here is another reference to the transfiguration as Jesus' true nature, and in this case the resurrection is presented as the revealing of his true self. Speaking of himself in the third person, Jesus says, "He has no human form, for whoever has a human form is the creation of another. And he has a semblance of his own, not like what you have seen and received, but a strange semblance that surpasses all things and is better than the universe. . . . He is imperishable and has no likeness."[54] The point here is that he could not have a body, since that would mean he was born, that he was the product of human procreation, which is condemned. Sex is considered an enslavement to the material world and is described as the "unclean rubbing," unworthy of the Savior.[55] Furthermore he could not have a birth because that would imply he must also have a death. Therefore, he is not like humans; he has no humanity or even human form.

The Testimony of Truth. The last of our anonymous documents, it is not entirely clear that The Testimony of Truth belongs in the docetic category. The reader is told that in his coming down to "hades" (earth), Christ "clothed himself with their first-fruits."[56] This seems to point to a hybrid christology with a tangible body. Indeed, some scholars have seen the influence of Valentinianism.[57] On the other hand, Christ is described as coming into the world (descending) at the Jordan River, reminiscent of the Marcionite "appearance" of an adult Jesus.[58] Also,

---

[53]The Sophia of Jesus Christ (in Robinson, *Nag Hammadi Library*, 222). It is unclear how an invisible spirit can "appear."

[54]Ibid., 224.

[55]Ibid., 221, 223, 235.

[56]The Testimony of Truth (in Robinson, *Nag Hammadi Library*, 451).

[57]Birger A. Pearson, introduction to The Testimony of Truth (in Robinson, *Nag Hammadi Library*, 448-49). Pearson speculates that the document may represent the teaching of Julius Cassianus, whom Clement of Alexandria said had "departed from the school of Valentinus." See Clement of Alexandria, *Stromateis* 3.8, 13, 91-92, 102. See also Davies, "Origins of Docetism," 24. If this theory is correct, we could have an example of the Eastern (docetic) faction of Valentinians. If, on the other hand, this document represents a hybrid christology, then we have a rare example of the combination of hybrid christology with asceticism.

[58]The Testimony of Truth (in Robinson, *Nag Hammadi Library*, 450; cf. 454, where there is mention of a birth through the Virgin Mary. While the mention of any birth at all might point to something closer to a hybrid christology, the fact that it is a virgin birth sets Jesus apart from humanity and becomes a condemnation of all sexuality).

the author criticizes Valentinians and others in the Hybrid Gnosticism camp, especially for their practice of a baptism (which, to a certain extent, acknowledges the human body).[59]

Ultimately Christ is described as having "destroyed the flesh," as evidenced by his ability to walk on water.[60] The point seems to be that human flesh is beneath him, and his own "flesh" is not really material or earthly flesh but an incorporeal substance. That human flesh is not worthy of Christ is demonstrated in the affirmation that his coming is meant to put an end to "carnal procreation."[61] The concept of a bodily resurrection is rejected as "destruction."[62] The document is clearly the product of an ascetic community that demands celibacy for its members.[63]

Cerdo and Marcion. Neither Cerdo nor Marcion can be called gnostics since they do not have the elaborate cosmologies of gnosticism nor do they have a soteriology that includes secret knowledge.[64] Therefore, for them, Christ is not the bringer of specific knowledge per se, though he does bring enlightenment. As we will see, however, their christology was the epitome of true docetism.

Irenaeus puts Cerdo in Rome in the 130s CE.[65] Cerdo, also called Cerdon, taught the kind of dualism that we normally associate with docetism: that matter is inherently evil.[66] He taught that the God of the Old Testament who created the world was a different God from the Father of Jesus. Christ came as a spiritual entity who "was not in

---

[59]The Testimony of Truth (in Robinson, *Nag Hammadi Library*, 452).

[60]Ibid., 451. The text in question is fragmented, and the meaning will depend on how one fills in the blanks.

[61]Ibid., 450.

[62]Ibid., 451-52.

[63]Ibid., 457.

[64]Peter Head, "The Foreign God and the Sudden Christ: Theology and Christology in Marcion's Gospel Redaction," *Tyndale Bulletin* 44, no. 2 (1993): 314. On Cerdo and Marcion, see Epiphanius, *Panarion* 41-42.

[65]Irenaeus of Lyons, *Against Heresies* 3.4.3; Eusebius of Caesarea, *Ecclesiastical History* 4.10-11. See also the chart titled "The Gnostic Family Tree," in Papandrea, *Reading the Early Church Fathers*, 231.

[66]Irenaeus of Lyons, *Against Heresies* 1.5.4; 1.27.1-2; Hippolytus, *Refutation of All Heresies* 10.15; pseudo-Tertullian, *Against All Heresies* 6; Eusebius of Caesarea, *Ecclesiastical History* 4.10-11.

the substance of flesh" but was rather "only in a phantasmal shape."[67] He had no birth and no passion.[68]

Marcion, the more famous student of Cerdo, continued and expanded on his teachings.[69] "While morbidly brooding over the question of the origin of evil," he became convinced that Cerdo's dualism was the answer.[70] The wealthy son of a bishop, he had come to Rome around the year 140 CE.[71] In 144, he was excommunicated by Bishop Pius I.[72] He continued teaching outside the authority of the bishop, gained followers and founded a movement that outlived him.

Marcion's editing of the apostolic documents is well known, but the point for our purposes is that for him Jesus could not be the Christ, because "Christ" was the title of the awaited Messiah of the Jews.[73] Although his critics were not always clear on this, I will use only the name "Jesus" to refer to Marcion's Savior. Thus Jesus is not the Son of the Old Testament God. For him, Jesus was entirely spiritual.[74] This Jesus was never born but simply appeared on earth in about the year 30 CE (at the beginning of Luke 3).[75]

Marcion apparently compared the body of Jesus to the angels who appeared to Abraham in Genesis 18. Like them, he believed that Jesus

---

[67] Pseudo-Tertullian, *Against All Heresies* 6.

[68] Ibid.

[69] Irenaeus of Lyons, *Against Heresies* 1.27.2; 3.4.3; Tertullian, *Against Marcion* 1.22; 3.21; 4.17; Hippolytus, *Refutation of All Heresies* 10.15; pseudo-Tertullian, *Against All Heresies* 6; Eusebius of Caesarea, *Ecclesiastical History* 4.10-11; Davies, "Origins of Docetism," 29.

[70] Tertullian, *Against Marcion* 1.2.

[71] Tertullian knows of a story which says that Marcion came to Rome with a letter of recommendation testifying to his orthodoxy. Tertullian, *Against Marcion* 1.1; 4.4; *On the Flesh of Christ* 2. On the other hand, many believed that he was already teaching dualism/docetism and had already been confronted by Polycarp in his letter to the Philippians. See Polycarp, *Letter to the Philippians* 7; Irenaeus of Lyons, *Against Heresies* 3.3.4. See also Head, "Foreign God," 309.

[72] Pseudo-Tertullian, *Against All Heresies* 6. See Head, "Foreign God," 309, esp. n. 7, on the dating of Marcion's career. Marcion was still alive when Justin wrote his first apology, Justin Martyr, *1 Apology* 26.

[73] Marcion rejected from his canon any documents (or parts of documents) that connected Jesus to the Old Testament, as fulfillment of prophecy, or even as agent of the Creator. It is noteworthy that Marcion seems to be the only author in the early church who rejected the Pastoral Epistles.

[74] Head, "Foreign God," 311-12. Cf. Carter, "Marcion's Christology," 552-53.

[75] Hippolytus, *Refutation of All Heresies* 7.19; 10.15; Tertullian, *Against Marcion* 3.8; 4.7; 4.21. See also Tertullian, *On the Flesh of Christ* 1-4; and Head, "Foreign God," 316, esp. n. 40.

appeared "in a phantom state, that of merely putative [supposed] flesh."[76] The point is that for Marcion the "body" of Jesus was only imaginary.[77] Therefore Jesus did not suffer, and his resurrection was not the resurrection of a body.[78] The asceticism of the Marcionites is well known and is consistent with his docetic christology.

Saturninus and the Encratites. Saturninus, also called Saturnilus, is said to be a disciple of Menander.[79] Like Menander, Saturninus taught that the Savior was unbegotten. According to Hippolytus,

---

[76]Tertullian, *Against Marcion* 3.9. Cf. Tertullian, *On the Flesh of Christ* 3. See Head, "Foreign God," 313.

[77]Tertullian, *Against Marcion* 3.8; Head, "Foreign God," 313, 316. Like the other docetics, Marcion interpreted the words "form" and "likeness" in Phil 2:7 in a docetic sense.

[78]Tertullian, *On the Flesh of Christ* 5; *Against Marcion* 3.8; 4.43; Head, "Foreign God," 321; and see Carter, "Marcion's Christology," for a detailed discussion of Marcion's alteration of Lk 24:39. It does appear, however, that Marcion accepted the idea of a death (and possibly even burial) of Jesus. Without the soteriology of knowledge of the gnostics, Marcion apparently felt he could not completely abandon the concept of an atonement. See Head, "Foreign God," 320; and see Tertullian, *On the Flesh of Christ* 5; *Against Marcion* 3.8; and Epiphanius, *Panarion* 42. Tertullian (and Epiphanius) pointed out the contradiction of rejecting the flesh while accepting the death; however, in *Against Marcion* 3.8 he seems to say that Marcion rejected the death of Jesus as well.

[79]According to the ancient sources, Menander, in turn, was supposedly a disciple of Simon Magus (of Acts 8:9-24). See Justin Martyr, *1 Apology* 26. Justin called him "Meander." See also Irenaeus of Lyons, *Against Heresies* 1.23.5; and Hippolytus, *Refutation of All Heresies* 6.2-15; 10.8. See also Epiphanius, *Panarion* 22. Justin Martyr tells us that both Simon and Menander were Samaritans and that Menander ended up in Antioch, where he dazzled people and gained a following by the use of magic. It appears that he was in Antioch during the time that Ignatius was bishop. See Pétrement, *A Separate God*, 319, 322; and Grant, "Earliest Christian Gnosticism," 81. However, upon closer examination, there does not seem to be enough of a discernable connection between what Simon is said to have taught and the teaching of Menander—other than the fact that they are both accused of practicing magic. See Grant, "Earliest Christian Gnosticism," 82-83, 87-88. On the other hand, both Simon and Menander were accused of teaching that they were the savior, though at least in the case of Menander it seems more likely that this is a later teaching of his disciples, after he was no longer around. See Pétrement, *A Separate God*, 320. A similar case would be that of Montanus, whose later followers (under Miltiades) said that he *was* the Holy Spirit rather than simply the mouthpiece of the Holy Spirit. Therefore, not much can be said with any confidence about Simon, and so he has been omitted from the present study. Though there were apparently "Simonians" within the church in the time of Justin, Simon and his followers must be kept in the category of "illusory early figures," along with the Nicolaitans (Rev 2:6, 15) and Hymenaeus and Philetus (2 Tim 2:17-18). In my opinion, it is more likely that Menander was a disciple of the latter two (based in part on his promise that his followers would never die), though this could hardly be proven. In any case, while the connection between Simon and Menander may be legendary, the connection between Menander and Saturninus seems to have more basis in fact. See Hippolytus, *Refutation of All Heresies* 8.13; Eusebius of Caesarea, *Ecclesiastical History* 4.7, 28-29; Epiphanius, *Panarion* 23, 47; and Pétrement, *A Separate God*, 334.

Saturninus's Christ was "unbegotten and incorporeal, and devoid of figure."[80] This is clearly more than saying he had a spiritual body; this is to say that he had no body at all—he was visible, but not tangible.[81]

Saturninus's dualism led him to the conclusion that all participation in flesh was beneath the truly spiritual person. He condemned marriage, saying that marriage and procreation are a creation of Satan.[82] He advocated vegetarianism and probably rejected the use of wine in his communion liturgy. His followers came to be known as the Encratites, and in addition to requiring celibacy, they were vegetarians and teetotalers.[83]

Summary and Implications

The truly docetic Christ is immaterial, incorporeal and intangible.[84] He did not come bearing a "luminous" or "ethereal" body as in the teachings of Hybrid Gnosticism—he had no body at all.[85] If he appeared to have a body, that was an illusion.[86] He was shapeless and formless but usually had the appearance of a human body, though sometimes he was invisible.[87] When he walked, he left no footprints.[88] The Sophia of Jesus Christ implies that some believed he was visible before the "resurrection" and invisible afterward.[89] According to the Acts of Andrew, he was translucent.

---

[80]Hippolytus, *Refutation of All Heresies* 7.16. This is quoted in Grant, "Earliest Christian Gnosticism," 89, where "devoid of figure" is translated "formless."

[81]Irenaeus of Lyons, *Against Heresies* 1.24.2; pseudo-Tertullian, *Against All Heresies* 1. See also Hippolytus, *Refutation of All Heresies* 7.16.

[82]Irenaeus of Lyons, *Against Heresies* 1.24.2. See also Hippolytus, *Refutation of All Heresies* 7.16; Davies, "Origins of Docetism," 20; and Grant, "Earliest Christian Gnosticism," 88.

[83]Although the origin of the Encratites is also attributed to both Marcion and Tatian, the mostly likely source is Saturninus. See Irenaeus of Lyons, *Against Heresies* 1.28.1; Hippolytus, *Refutation of All Heresies* 8.13. Cf. Eusebius of Caesarea, *Ecclesiastical History* 4.7, 28. See also Davies, "Origins of Docetism," 34, for some speculation on the connection between the Encratites and the apocryphal acts, such as the Acts of Peter.

[84]The Concept of Our Great Power 44 (in Robinson, *Nag Hammadi Library*, 314); Acts of John 93, 107. The Acts of John says that sometimes he was tangible, though sometimes he felt soft to the touch and other times he felt hard.

[85]Acts of John 102.

[86]Tertullian, *Against Marcion* 3.8-9.

[87]Hippolytus, *Refutation of All Heresies* 7.16; 10.12; Acts of John 98; The Sophia of Jesus Christ (in Robinson, *Nag Hammadi Library*, 224).

[88]Acts of John 93.

[89]The Sophia of Jesus Christ (in Robinson, *Nag Hammadi Library*, 222).

All of this was apparently maintained in order to preserve the immutability, impassibility and incorruptibility of Christ, since these divine attributes were held to be incompatible with humanity. In addition, the dualistic conviction that the flesh (being material) was a product of an evil Creator and part of an evil world led to the need to quarantine the Savior in the realm of the purely spiritual. For some in the early church, including Cerdo, Marcion and Saturninus (and possibly Menander), no concession could be made to the canonical witness to Jesus' humanity. Along with these heresiarchs, the purely docetic christology can be detected in the authors of the Acts of John, the Acts of Andrew, the Nag Hammadi documents known as The Concept of Our Great Power and The Sophia of Jesus Christ, and possibly also in The Testimony of Truth as well as the Thomas tradition that includes the Gospel of Thomas, the Acts of Thomas and The Book of Thomas the Contender. However, it must be acknowledged that we are not trying to demonstrate a complete agreement among these sources. No doubt there was more of a continuum of christology than a limited number of pigeonholes. Nevertheless, it is clear that a purely docetic understanding of Christ existed within the early church and continued to exist alongside the less docetic Hybrid Gnosticism, even after the latter evolved from it.

The docetic Christ was described as unbegotten because those in the camp of Docetic Gnosticism believed that to say he was begotten meant that he could not be divine—one who is begotten, they reasoned, must be created, mutable, corruptible and ultimately mortal.[90] However, by rejecting the generation of the Son, they logically lost the distinction from the Father, creating a kind of gnostic modalism.

Docetic christology also has implications for anthropology. By denying any identification of the Savior with humanity, Marcion and others like him taught that only the spiritual part of a person could be

---

[90]The concept of eternal generation was the mainstream church's solution to the problem. Novatian and others after him understood Christ to be both eternal (thus equal to the Father in divinity) and begotten (thus distinct from the Father, avoiding modalism). See James L. Papandrea, *Novatian of Rome and the Culmination of Pre-Nicene Orthodoxy*, Princeton Theological Monographs 175 (Eugene, OR: Pickwick, 2011), 85-92.

saved—the body could not be.[91] This meant that the human body was not really a part of the person, but was disposable and to be despised—a perspective that Irenaeus rejected.[92]

As I have noted, there is a connection between docetism and asceticism, and it appears that the more docetic one's christology was, the more ascetic one's lifestyle was likely to be.[93] The belief that matter is evil naturally led to the conclusion that the human body is evil.[94] Denigration of the body led to a disgust, and so for the true docetics, aversion led to avoidance. Whereas Hybrid Gnosticism led to a *flaunting* of the physical through a hedonistic lifestyle, the purely docetic christology tended toward a *rejection* of the physical through an ascetic lifestyle. Therefore marriage and sexuality were condemned as part of the fallen state of humanity. To "be fruitful and multiply" would be to collaborate with the Old Testament God or perhaps to participate in the attempts of lesser deities who try to create out of preexisting matter.[95] The docetics also pushed to the extreme the idea that women were responsible for the lust of men, and they made women out to be the very embodiment of sin.[96] Since animal flesh was also evil, the ascetic lifestyle included vegetarianism.[97]

Finally, it should be noted that both the anthropology and the lifestyle that would be consistent with docetic christology led its adherents to neglect the needs of the poor. Docetism, as a dualism that separates spirit from matter, also separates faith from works, making

---

[91]Irenaeus of Lyons, *Against Heresies* 1.27.3; Head, "Foreign God," 313.

[92]Irenaeus of Lyons, *Against Heresies* 5.2, 6.

[93]For the connection between docetic christology and asceticism, see Clement of Alexandria, *Stromateis* 3.13. As with the christology, so with the lifestyle—we cannot assume complete agreement across the board or that everyone's behavior was logically consistent with their christology (or that of their leader). It is not impossible that there was some libertinism among the true docetics (and we have no idea what people really did behind closed doors), but logic and the primary sources do point to a certain consistency. See Grant, "Earliest Christian Gnosticism," 94; and Gunther, "Syrian Christian Dualism," 88.

[94]Davies, "Origins of Docetism," 20.

[95]Gunther, "Syrian Christian Dualism," 88.

[96]Grant, "Earliest Christian Gnosticism," 89; Igino Giordani, *The Social Message of the Early Christians*, trans. Alba I. Zizzamia (Boston: The Daughters of St. Paul, 1977), 326-27.

[97]Tertullian, *Against Marcion* 1.14. Tertullian implies that Marcion allowed the eating of fish. See Gunther, "Syrian Christian Dualism," 87. It may be that there was a connection between vegetarianism and reincarnation, which some of the docetics seem to have accepted. On reincarnation, see Irenaeus of Lyons, *Against Heresies* 1.23.2.

works irrelevant. To be dispassionate in the Stoic sense easily becomes a lack of compassion. Whereas the orthodox incarnation teaches of the divine Son that comes into the world of people, docetism teaches of the removal of people from the world, and with that, the removal of all responsibility toward one's neighbor.[98]

---

[98]Ignatius of Antioch, *Letter to the Smyrnaeans* 6.2. See also Rhee, *Loving the Poor*, 173-74; and Giordani, *Social Message of the Early Christians*, 324.

5

CHRIST AS COSMIC MIND

Hybrid Gnosticism

The traditional wisdom has been that the gnosticism of the second century evolved from earlier docetics, or "proto-gnostics," and is the result of the syncretism of various pagan mythologies with the docetics' extreme version of Platonic dualism. The evidence of these earlier docetics can be seen in such New Testament passages as 1 John 4:2-3. These docetics, it is assumed, held such a radical dualism that they did not believe it was possible for the divine and purely spiritual Christ to come into contact with the material world. In other words, the Word could not become flesh.

However, the issue of materiality was not necessarily a matter of either/or in the ancient world. It is not necessarily the case that we can say anything was thought to be entirely nonmaterial. On the contrary, there seems to have been an assumption of degrees of materiality.[1] Athanasius tells us in the *Life of Antony* that demons have "more subtle bodies than we have."[2] That is, these purely spiritual beings are nevertheless material—just "thinner" and "lighter" than our human bodies. In addition to this, the majority of gnostic texts available to us do not portray a Christ who was completely incorporeal

---

[1]Similarly, gnostics assumed that there were also degrees of divinity. Some deities were more divine than others, and some deities were "created" in the sense that they were the product of cosmic procreation (pairs of deities begetting new deities), which means that gnostics did not assume divinity necessarily meant eternality.

[2]Athanasius, *Life of Antony* 31.

(that is to say, intangible), as the Christ of the docetics was. Rather, when we listen to most gnostic sources, we hear of a Jesus who was in fact tangible and who had a "luminous" or "ethereal" "body" made of a spiritual element.[3] A perfect example of this is the Infancy Gospel of Thomas, which tells of a Jesus who could be bumped into (with disastrous results).[4]

While I am reluctant to completely abandon the assumption that gnosticism in general is based on an extreme dualism, nevertheless many gnostics apparently could not ignore the ubiquitous witnesses to the tangible presence of Jesus. For one thing, there are simply too many stories in which he ate. What I am proposing is that, alongside the purely Docetic Gnosticism, there also developed a "hybrid" Gnosticism, a combination of a purer docetism with a concession to the mainstream affirmation of Jesus' bodily existence.[5] It was as if most gnostics eventually said that he may not have been human (that would be too much to take), but it appears that he was tangible. He may not have been as material as we are (for that would imply that the Christ was fallen), but he was not completely incorporeal. The very concept of a Hybrid Gnosticism may seem like a redundancy, as though I am saying these gnostics were syncretistic syncretists, but that is precisely the point. These gnostics were probably looking for a happy medium between pure docetism and mainstream Christianity, perhaps as a way to move closer to the majority and avoid schism. If this is the case, we have to be careful with how we use the Nag Hammadi Library as evidence for early christology, since these documents are the result of a century or two of syncretism and concession to the mainstream.

Hybrid christology is in fact a kind of gnostic adoptionism. It begins with the separation of Jesus from the Christ in order to allow a certain tangibility of Jesus, while preserving the Christ as a purely

---

[3]David E. Hahm, "The Fifth Element in Aristotle's *De Philosophia*: A Critical Re-Examination," *Journal of Hellenic Studies* 102 (1982): 60, 68, 71.

[4]Though the boy Jesus is tangible in this document, he is nevertheless described as "not of this earth" and a god or an angel (of God). See Infancy Gospel of Thomas 7, 17.

[5]I first suggested this category of Hybrid Gnosticism in my book *Reading the Early Church Fathers: From the Didache to Nicaea* (Mahwah, NJ: Paulist Press, 2012), 58-77.

spiritual entity. Thus "Jesus" is the disguise worn by the Christ, similar to the indwelling of Angel Adoptionism.[6] The difference between Hybrid Gnosticism and Angel Adoptionism is that for the gnostics, the one who appears as Jesus is not really human but rather a semitangible being posing as a human. Thus he is only one of us in the sense that we have the potential to become what he is, but the connection between Jesus and humanity is still more of an illusion than a reality.

Admittedly, it is no more accurate to present Hybrid Gnosticism as a unified sect than it is to present all of gnosticism as a unified sect. Therefore we will see a certain diversity of expression within and among the groups in this category. In some cases, scholars have even debated whether they should be called gnostic at all. Nevertheless, the category will, I trust, prove helpful in our overall exploration of early christologies. Within the category that I am calling Hybrid Gnosticism, the propensity to personify and deify every conceivable philosophical concept means that the Christ will go by many different names. Various gnostic cosmologies refer to the divine entity as the Christ, Son, Logos, Savior and other names, including *Nous* (Mind). There is also a variety of myths about the origin of this divine entity, but the common denominator seems to be that he is a rational emanation from the divine realm, divine but not eternal in that he is the product of cosmic procreation. Therefore he is considered both divine and created, an impossibility to the mind of most Christians. He was sent to humanity to bring "secret knowledge," that is, the illumination that comes from the awareness of the gnostic myth(s) and of each person's internal divinity.

The problem is that the various names for Christ sometimes refer to different entities within the same cosmology and at other times are multiple names for the same entity. Strictly speaking, it is not necessary to sort out the different names for the Christ in order to understand gnostic christology, so we will leave that aside for the present study and simply say that in general, for Hybrid Gnosticism, the

---

[6]Tertullian, *Against the Valentinians* 27.

Christ is a cosmic mind that comes to inhabit the "man" known as Jesus. For example, in the Valentinian version, the Christ is the pre-existent rationality that inspires and empowers the (not preexistent) Jesus.[7] Some seem to have believed that the Christ was in fact the Father or the hypostatized *name* of the Father, implying that it was the Father who came disguised as the Son.[8]

THE CHRISTOLOGY OF HYBRID GNOSTICISM

Hybrid Gnosticism differs from Docetic Gnosticism in that here the man called Jesus is not simply an illusion but material being with a tangible body. However, that body is still not a human body since it is made of something like ether, which is described in ancient sources as a "luminous," fiery substance, or a divine substance.[9] Therefore the body of Jesus, although it is distinct from the cosmic mind (the Christ) that inhabits it, is in some sense a divine body, and although it is tangible, it is most certainly not human.[10] If anything, it may be that some gnostics believed it to be made of the same substance as human souls, but only because they believed human souls to be divine sparks trapped within the world of matter.[11] Some, like Carpocrates and Cerinthus, apparently allowed that Jesus even came into the world in the usual way, born of a man and a woman. Others said that he "passed through Mary just as water flows through a tube."[12] Some apparently believed that he was able

---

[7]J. Zandee, "Gnostic Ideas on the Fall and Salvation," *Numen* 11, no. 1 (1964): 52. See, e.g., the Infancy Gospel of Thomas 7, in which the boy Jesus is described as "born before the creation of the world" and "before all ages" (in the second Greek and Latin versions).

[8]Zandee, "Gnostic Ideas," 52-53. Note the affinity with modalism, which will be addressed in the concluding chapter.

[9]Hahm, "Fifth Element," 61, 63, 68.

[10]Irenaeus of Lyons, *Against Heresies* 1.6. Others have called this body a "psychic" body or a "pneumatic" body. See Zandee, "Gnostic Ideas," 64. However, the point is that the body of Jesus is not a real human body; it is on some level of materiality that is between purely docetic and fully human. See Gregory A. Smith, "How Thin Is a Demon?", *Journal of Early Christian Studies* 16, no. 4 (2008): 481-82, 484-86, 488.

[11]Hahm, "Fifth Element," 64, 66.

[12]Irenaeus of Lyons, *Against Heresies* 1.7.2. Irenaeus uses the term "Christ" to mean the corporeal Jesus, which, he goes on to say, the gnostics believed was later indwelt by the Savior, who descended on him at his baptism in the form of a dove. Both the Protevangelium of James and the Ascension of Isaiah contain elements of a "docetic" birth of Christ, which acknowledges the birth itself but suggests that Mary suffered no pain and Jesus emerged from her like a beam of light.

to suffer and die on the cross, but most believed that he was not and that his passion was an illusion. However, those who believed that the tangible Jesus could suffer would still have kept the extreme separation between Jesus and the Christ that would protect the cosmic mind from any suffering.[13]

Thus the relationship between the divine Christ and the "man" Jesus was one in which the Christ "put on Jesus" and "bore him."[14] In other words, the Christ wears Jesus like a garment. Therefore, to speak of Christ being "in the flesh" does not mean the same thing as John's "the Word became flesh." Rather, it means that Christ entered the tangible realm by putting on a body that was not fully human.[15] Thus there is still a docetic element in the hybrid Jesus in the sense that "the flesh" refers to the outward appearance of humanity only.[16]

Like Angel Adoptionism, this form of gnostic christology assumes that whatever indwelling existed is temporary, either from the birth or the baptism of Jesus to the cross.[17] Some specifically said that the Christ left Jesus at the moment he met Pontius Pilate.[18] Although he calls it docetic, Hippolytus described the hybrid christology as one in which the Christ was "clothed in darkness" (i.e., corporeality) from birth but his body was stripped off to be nailed to the cross.[19] Thus part of the mission of the Christ come to earth is to show the way of ascent out of the prison of the body.[20]

---

[13]Irenaeus of Lyons, *Against Heresies* 1.6-7. The divine Christ was immutable and could not suffer.

[14]Trimorphic Protennoia (in James M. Robinson, ed., *The Nag Hammadi Library in English* [1978; repr., San Francisco: HarperSanFrancisco, 1990], 521). See also Zandee, "Gnostic Ideas," 64.

[15]Zandee, "Gnostic Ideas," 64. By "fully" human, I mean having a full human nature, with a human mind and will, and being consubstantial with humanity.

[16]Ibid., 65. For example, while the Infancy Gospel of Thomas portrays a Jesus who is tangible, his humanity is diminished by the fact that his miraculous abilities are fully developed in his childhood. The idea that he "grew and became strong" (Lk 2:40) is rejected in favor of a latent docetism.

[17]Irenaeus of Lyons, *Against Heresies* 1.7.2; Tertullian, *Against the Valentinians* 27.

[18]Irenaeus of Lyons, *Against Heresies* 1.7.

[19]Hippolytus, *Refutation of All Heresies* 8.3.

[20]Zandee, "Gnostic Ideas," 64.

THE MAJOR PROPONENTS AND THEIR PRIMARY DOCUMENTS

The Carpocratians. Carpocrates is said to have taught that Jesus was a man who was born of Mary and Joseph but whose soul remembered its prebirth existence. This allowed him to become the most righteous man who ever lived, since he was able to remember the truth about creation and despise the Creator. This is clearly a syncretism of docetic dualism with Christianity and Platonic reincarnation. As a reward for his righteousness, the power of (the higher) God descended on Jesus at his baptism, and he "became" the Christ.[21] The followers of Carpocrates expected that they, too, would earn the right to become christs.[22]

That the Carpocratians were said to be hedonists is well known.[23] But for Irenaeus, their real problem was relativism.[24] In other words, they believed that nothing was good or evil in and of itself, but that human opinion made it so. Thus in throwing off human opinion, they were free to engage in any behavior without any need for self-control. It is this "throwing off" of human values that I would argue is directly related to a christology in which the transcendent Christ "throws off" the garment of a body to reveal his true (free) self.

Cerinthus. Like Carpocrates, Cerinthus taught that Jesus was not born of a virgin but came into the world as the son of Mary and Joseph. The divine Christ descended on him in the form of a dove at his baptism but left him just before he went to the cross.[25] Thus Jesus suffered alone; the Christ did not suffer. Jesus was raised, though it is not clear what sort of resurrection Cerinthus envisioned.[26] The document known as the Apocryphon of James may be a Cerinthian text.[27] In it, a resurrected Jesus refers to the ascension as stripping himself.[28] In other words, whatever kind of body he was thought to have in his earthly life may have been raised from the dead, but it was not a

---

[21]Irenaeus of Lyons, *Against Heresies* 1.25; Hippolytus, *Refutation of All Heresies* 7.20. See also Epiphanius, *Panarion* 26-27.

[22]Hippolytus, *Refutation of All Heresies* 7.22.

[23]See, e.g., Clement of Alexandria, *Stromateis* 3.

[24]Irenaeus of Lyons, *Against Heresies* 1.25.4.

[25]Irenaeus of Lyons, *Against Heresies* 1.7.2.

[26]Hippolytus, *Refutation of All Heresies* 7.20. See also Epiphanius, *Panarion* 28.

[27]Robinson, *Nag Hammadi Library*, 29.

[28]Apocryphon of James (in Robinson, *Nag Hammadi Library*, 36).

humanity that was an essential part of his personhood or that would accompany him to heaven. For the gnostics, salvation was not for the body.[29] Thus while the Carpocratians and Cerinthians did not overtly deny the humanity of Jesus (causing some early commentators to describe them as adoptionists), they did believe and teach that whatever part of him was corporeal, this was not the essence of him, but was rather something to be shed.

Basilides. According to Basilides, Christ is the *Nous* (cosmic Mind) inhabiting Jesus.[30] Because the coming of the Christ into Jesus was foreknown at creation, his birth could be foretold with the star of Bethlehem.[31] The death of Jesus demonstrates a dualistic separation of matter and spirit, such that his resurrection was only the resuscitation of his body.[32] This is evident in the fact that the Christ left Jesus before the cross and did not return to him. In some versions of the story, the Christ switches bodies with Simon of Cyrene, who was conscripted to carry the cross and, in a Monty Python–like irony, got stuck with it. The Christ stands by laughing while the wrong man is crucified.[33]

Because of this "laughing Jesus" motif, it is possible that the document known as the Apocalypse of Peter is the product of a disciple of Basilides. In the Apocalypse of Peter, we can see a distinction between the "*Living* Jesus" (i.e., the Christ) and the "fleshy part," who is the "substitute" who was nailed to the cross in humiliation.[34] The Living Jesus is called the Savior and is associated with the Holy Spirit. He is surrounded by "ineffable light."[35] Though he is said to be "on the tree," he laughs there to show that he is not affected by the crucifixion

---

[29]Irenaeus of Lyons, *Against Heresies* 1.24.5; Tertullian, *On the Flesh of Christ* 10; *Against the Valentinians* 26.

[30]Irenaeus of Lyons, *Against Heresies* 1.24. See also Epiphanius, *Panarion* 24; 44.1-4; and Eusebius of Caesarea, *Ecclesiastical History* 4.7.

[31]Hippolytus, *Refutation of All Heresies* 7.15.

[32]Ibid.

[33]Irenaeus of Lyons, *Against Heresies* 1.24.4. On the laughing Christ, see Robert M. Grant, "Gnostic Origins and the Basilidians of Irenaeus," *Vigiliae Christianae* 13, no. 2 (1959): 123. Grant proposes that this concept of Christ laughing may be related to a particular exegesis of Ps 2:4.

[34]Apocalypse of Peter (in Robinson, *Nag Hammadi Library*, 376-78).

[35]Ibid., 377.

and does not suffer. He also laughs at the ignorance of those who tried to crucify him.[36] The "fleshy part," on the other hand, is described as the *likeness* of the Living Jesus but is a vessel (for the Living Jesus to inhabit) and is under the law (as opposed to being associated with the Spirit).[37]

To summarize these early versions of Hybrid Gnosticism, they have rejected the more mainstream (i.e., Johannine) idea that Jesus of Nazareth was divine by nature and proposed that divinity was rather infused into him, which warrants the description as a kind of "gnostic adoptionism." What makes them gnostic, however, is that the "human" element, Jesus, becomes progressively less human over time, so that by the time of Basilides, his body is simply a vessel or a disguise. The inhabitation of divinity in the tangible body of Jesus is only temporary, and the dualism we are used to ascribing to all gnostics is still evident in the fact that there is no ontological contact of the spiritual with the material. The body of Jesus is merely an ethereal (that is, less material than a truly human body) garment worn by the *Nous*, or a vessel, but is not part of the essence of the Christ. The body may be raised, but only to be shed, and so it does not ascend. Thus it is disdained and will not be included in salvation. The Christ is a divine entity who only inhabits the body of Jesus and, in gnostic teaching, is kept separate from Jesus, probably as a way to preserve the immutability of the divine spirit.[38]

The Sethians. What we call Sethian gnosticism represents a range of gnostic beliefs; however, we can summarize their christology because we have several documents that scholars have grouped together under the Sethian umbrella.[39] Like the groups we have looked at so far, the Sethians taught that *Nous* (the Christ, who is apparently also the Seth of Gen 4:25–5:8) "put on" Jesus like a garment, or inhabited

---

[36]Ibid.

[37]Ibid.

[38]Simone Pétrement, *A Separate God: The Origins and Teachings of Gnosticism* (San Francisco: HarperSanFrancisco, 1990), 146-47, 150. Pétrement argues that the desire to preserve the immutability of the divine was the primary motivation, and the dualistic aversion to creation was only secondary.

[39]See the list of Sethian documents in Nicola Denzey Lewis, *Introduction to "Gnosticism": Ancient Voices, Christian Worlds* (Oxford: Oxford University Press, 2013), 121.

him, making him little more than a vessel.[40] In the document known as the Trimorphic Protennoia, Christ says, "As for me, I put on Jesus."[41] The Christ is also said to prevent Jesus from suffering, as the Christ "carries him away from the crucifixion." In the Gospel of Judas, Jesus (speaking for the *Nous* within him) refers to his body as "the man that clothes me." However, unlike the groups we have seen so far, the Sethians accepted the idea of a virgin birth, which for them is what makes the vessel pure enough to hold the Christ spirit.[42]

In the document known as the Second Treatise of the Great Seth, the crucifixion account is influenced by the Basilidean "laughing Jesus." Simon of Cyrene is crucified as Christ laughs, saying, "I did not die in reality, but in appearance."[43] Jesus was raised, but his resurrection was that of a cosmic body, not a "mundane" (earthly) body.[44] In the Apocryphon of John, Adam is said to have originally had a luminous body. Out of jealousy, the heavenly powers entombed him in a human body and in "the bond of forgetfulness."[45] The implication is that the body of Jesus is a body like Adam originally had, while the rest of us are imprisoned in heavier, more material bodies. In Jesus, then, the Christ (called *Pronoia*) "entered into the midst of their prison, which is the prison of the body." He did this to bring back the memory of what Adam had forgotten.[46]

The Valentinians. Valentinus founded what would become the most well-known form of gnosticism.[47] Just like their understanding of Christ, the Valentinian gnostics believed that they were in their essence

---

[40]Ibid., 173.

[41]Trimorphic Protennoia (in Robinson, *Nag Hammadi Library*, 521). Note that there is some scholarly debate about this passage, with some speculating that it is a later addition to the text. See Lewis, *Introduction to "Gnosticism,"* 199.

[42]Irenaeus of Lyons, *Against Heresies* 1.30. See also Hippolytus, *Refutation of All Heresies* 5.14-17; and Epiphanius, *Panarion* 39-40. See note 12 in this chapter.

[43]Second Treatise of the Great Seth (in Robinson, *Nag Hammadi Library*, 365).

[44]Irenaeus of Lyons, *Against Heresies* 1.30.12-13. Irenaeus tells us that the Sethians used 1 Cor 15:50, "flesh and blood cannot inherit the kingdom of God," as a prooftext for the idea that the body could not be saved.

[45]Apocryphon of John (in Robinson, *Nag Hammadi Library*, 116-17). Note that the Son of Man is Seth (119). That the Apocryphon of John is Sethian, see Lewis, *Introduction to "Gnosticism,"* 121; and Michael Allen Williams, *Rethinking "Gnosticism": An Argument for Dismantling a Dubious Category* (Princeton: Princeton University Press, 1996), 13.

[46]Apocryphon of John (in Robinson, *Nag Hammadi Library*, 122). Irenaeus quotes from the Apocryphon of John in *Against Heresies* 1.29.

[47]See the chart "The Gnostic Family Tree" in Papandrea, *Reading the Early Church Fathers*, 231.

a divine spark trapped in a corporeal existence, which led them to refer to themselves as "Spirituals."[48] Therefore the Valentinians exemplified Hybrid Gnosticism in that the difference between Christ and the gnostic believer was not a difference between divinity and humanity (or two natures versus one), but a difference of what kind of body the divine spark found itself inhabiting. Christ was a divine spark inhabiting a luminous body; the Spirituals believed themselves to be divine sparks inhabiting human bodies. What separated the Spirituals from other humans, then, was their supposed awareness of their divinity. This awareness was apparently at least part of the knowledge (*gnōsis*) that the gnostics believed Jesus came to bring.

The Valentinian Gospel of Truth tells of the Word, called the Son and the Savior, who came from the highest heaven (the *plērōma*) to bring knowledge of the true Father.[49] In fact, the Son is the hypostatized name of the Father.[50] The Word "became a body," but that body was really only the appearance of flesh and is described as "perishable rags."[51] He was nailed to a tree, like an edict that is published by being nailed up in a public place, implying that his body is like the parchment of the edict. At the crucifixion, he "stripped himself of the perishable rags" and "put on imperishability."[52] However, Jesus did suffer, accepting his suffering "since he knew that his death was life for many."[53] Thus there is an element of atonement in the Valentinian concept of the crucifixion, demonstrating that Hybrid Gnosticism is a movement away from pure docetism toward mainstream Christianity (or perhaps a movement away from mainstream Christianity toward docetism).

---

[48]A Valentinian Exposition (in Robinson, *Nag Hammadi Library*, 485-86). The idea as expressed in this text sounds Pauline and may be based on Col 2:9 and/or Phil 2. In the Valentinian Exposition, the Son is the fullness of divinity and the agent of creation who left the realm of the powers to descend to the realm of humanity. See Irenaeus of Lyons, *Against Heresies* 2.32. See also Epiphanius, *Panarion* 31; and Eusebius of Caesarea, *Ecclesiastical History* 4.11.

[49]The Gospel of Truth (in Robinson, *Nag Hammadi Library*, 40).

[50]The Gospel of Truth (in Robinson, *Nag Hammadi Library*, 49). That the name is hypostatized, see Zandee, "Gnostic Ideas," 53.

[51]The Gospel of Truth (in Robinson, *Nag Hammadi Library*, 31, 42, 44).

[52]Ibid., 41-42.

[53]Ibid.

The Gospel of Philip, also a Valentinian text, includes a kind of gnostic "trinity" made up of the heavenly Father, the heavenly mother (the Holy Spirit) and their heavenly Son, Christ. Just as Jesus had an earthly father and mother in Joseph and Mary, the Christ has a heavenly Father and Mother.[54] The Gospel of Philip affirms the virgin birth of Jesus but says it could not have been accomplished by the Holy Spirit since the Holy Spirit is female, and two females (the Holy Spirit and Mary) could not conceive a child.[55] Jesus had flesh, but his body is called "contemptible."[56] Jesus did experience death, but the Christ did not. The cry of "Why have you forsaken me?" came at the very moment that the Christ left Jesus alone on the cross.[57]

It must be acknowledged that the Gospel of Philip contains a few elements that make us wonder whether the community that produced it was as hedonistic as the Valentinians were said to be.[58] First of all, there is a condemnation of adultery.[59] However, when read in context, the condemnation is not against extramarital sex per se, but rather against "sexual intercourse which has occurred between those unlike" (i.e., different from each other). The point is that this is probably more of a prohibition against relationships with non-Valentinians. At another point, physical marriage (as opposed to gnostic spiritual marriage) is called "marriage of defilement."[60] However, we know of gnostic sects who disparaged marriage while encouraging orgies, saying that the only reason *not* to have sex was procreation.[61] This attitude prompted some writers such as Clement of Alexandria to take the polar opposite approach.[62] Therefore, these two passages do not

---

[54]The Gospel of Philip (in Robinson, *Nag Hammadi Library*, 142-43). This gnostic "trinity" is also found in the Sethian document the Apocryphon of John (in Robinson, *Nag Hammadi Library*, 109).

[55]The Gospel of Philip (in Robinson, *Nag Hammadi Library*, 143, 152).

[56]Ibid., 144.

[57]Ibid., 144, 151.

[58]Tertullian, *Against the Valentinians* 30.

[59]The Gospel of Philip (in Robinson, *Nag Hammadi Library*, 146).

[60]The Gospel of Philip (in Robinson, *Nag Hammadi Library*, 158). Williams, *Rethinking "Gnosticism,"* 144, takes this as evidence of asceticism in the document. Lewis, *Introduction to "Gnosticism,"* 71, also believes this document is more docetic.

[61]Epiphanius, *Panarion* 26.4-5.

[62]Clement of Alexandria, *The Instructor* 10.

give us enough evidence of asceticism to assume that the lifestyle of the Gospel of Philip community was any different from those of the other Hybrid Gnostics.

The Treatise on the Resurrection says that the Lord embraced both divinity and humanity; however, it is clear that the humanity is embraced only temporarily, since his resurrection was the revealing of an already realized eschatology, in which the world is an illusion. The transfiguration is described as a moment when reality broke through the illusion. Therefore, although he had flesh, his visible (and tangible) body is discarded, and only that which was temporarily housed within it will ascend.[63]

The students of Valentinus continued the trajectory he was on, although Apelles denied the virgin birth of Jesus. He said that the body of Jesus was a cosmic body made up of cosmic elements. This body was raised (since Jesus was tangible after the resurrection), but it did not ascend with him into heaven; rather it dissolved back into the cosmic elements from which it was made.[64] Other students of Valentinus are said to have taught that Jesus was uniquely created in the likeness of the Christ to be the vessel that the Christ would indwell.[65]

SUMMARY AND IMPLICATIONS

The gnostic teachers and communities mentioned in this chapter have certain common elements with regard to their christology. To them, the Christ is a divine rationality (the *Nous*), a cosmic mind who is preexistent but who is nevertheless created by the procreation of other deities in the cosmic realm.[66] Therefore, he is not coeternal with the highest God, which makes him an intermediate divinity in a hierarchy of cosmic beings.[67] The *Nous* then inhabits a tangible Jesus, who is portrayed in the various systems as having a more or

---

[63]The Treatise on the Resurrection (in Robinson, *Nag Hammadi Library*, 54-56).

[64]Hippolytus, *Refutation of All Heresies* 7.26. See also Epiphanius, *Panarion* 44.

[65]Irenaeus of Lyons, *Against Heresies* 1.12-15. In the Letter of Ptolemy, Jesus seems to be a kind of offspring of Christ and the Holy Spirit. See Williams, *Rethinking "Gnosticism,"* 15.

[66]In many of the gnostic cosmologies, the various deities are described as existing in pairs of male and female, which procreate and bring new deities into existence. See also the Infancy Gospel of Thomas (Latin version, chap. 5), in which the boy Jesus is described as created.

[67]See Tertullian, *Against the Valentinians* 7.

less diminished humanity.[68] Sometimes he sounds quite human, but even then his human body is denigrated and discarded. The man Jesus is reduced to a garment of flesh worn by the divine *Nous* and is described in ways that seem to anticipate Apollinarius. That is, whatever humanity Jesus appears to have, it is not a full humanity because it is reduced to a disguise for the divine Christ to inhabit during his time on earth.

Furthermore, the union of the Christ and Jesus is neither natural nor permanent; thus it is not a "hypostatic" union in the later orthodox sense, but rather it is more like a Nestorian combination of the oil of divinity with the vinegar of matter. The two must eventually separate. By either duping Simon of Cyrene or simply abandoning Jesus, the Christ avoids the suffering of the cross. For some, Jesus did suffer and die, but for others he did not. Some said he was raised, and while it is unclear how this could be the case when Christ had already separated from Jesus before his suffering, the ascension of Christ is portrayed as a stripping off of the corporeal "rags" that he was "wearing." These rags of flesh (or the appearance of flesh) are then discarded and have no part in the Christ's ascent back to the heavens. In this way, proponents of Hybrid Gnosticism have separated the Christ from Jesus in order to allow that Jesus was tangible and to protect the Christ from suffering.[69] Even so, the body of Jesus is a cosmic body, corporeal but less material than a human body. Jesus is not truly human, because humanity (as a material existence) is ignoble and undesirable. The culmination of Christ's ministry of illumination is to strip off the "perishable rags" of the body and discard them.

In an effort to move away from lumping all of gnosticism into one category, I am proposing a subcategory, which I call "Hybrid" Gnosticism because it combines elements of docetism with an acknowledgment of the tangibility of Jesus as well as an occasional nod to the

---

[68]Some have argued that the Jesus of Cerinthus and Basilides was actually fully human; however, it probably only appears that way in comparison to pure docetism. Nevertheless, several of the early church critics (as well as a few modern commentators) seem confused about whether these heretics were gnostics or adoptionists. See Pétrement, *A Separate God*, 152-53; and Lewis, *Introduction to "Gnosticism,"* 71.

[69]Zandee, "Gnostic Ideas," 52.

atonement. It is a hybrid of Docetic Gnosticism with mainstream Christianity, but in a way it is also a hybrid of gnosticism with adoptionism, which creates what could also be seen as a kind of gnostic combination of Apollinarianism and Nestorianism in the sense that there is no full humanity and no real connection between the divine and the "human" (i.e., material) natures. The union of the Christ with Jesus is not an incarnation, nor even an indwelling, but a temporary inhabitation that does not extend all the way to death on the cross. Michael Allen Williams has remarked that Ptolemy's christology was the (Valentinian) gnostic solution to the paradox of Jesus Christ's suffering and death with his divinity.[70] I would expand that idea to say that all of the schools of gnostic thought that I take together as Hybrid Gnosticism were an attempt to reconcile the irrefutable tangibility of Jesus with the divinity of Christ. To do that, they distinguish Jesus and the Christ as two separate entities, making the tangibility possible on the one hand but protecting the immutability of the divine on the other. Also, there is still enough docetism in this christology that even the tangible body of Jesus is not a full humanity but rather only a garment of flesh, a "luminous," "ethereal" or "cosmic" body that is unlike our own.

Separating Jesus from the Christ makes the body of Jesus (and, it could be argued, the human body in general) little more than a corporeal garment to be worn by a spiritual being. Gnostic christology creates (or assumes) an anthropology which says that my body is not part of the essence of who I am. Instead, the human body is a prison to be escaped. The essence of a person is the divine spark within, completely apart from the body. This means that, as humans, we are more like the Christ than like Jesus.[71] In fact, the human soul is described as the bride of Christ, but also as the sister of Christ, the siblings being offspring of the same Father.[72] In the end, the body (whether cosmic or human) becomes disposable. And when it is disposable, it

---

[70]Williams, Rethinking "Gnosticism," 88-89.

[71]In gnostic belief, the divine spark within the human is consubstantial with the divine. See Birger A. Pearson, Ancient Gnosticism: Traditions and Literature (Minneapolis: Fortress, 2007), 13, 17.

[72]The Exegesis on the Soul (in Robinson, Nag Hammadi Library, 195).

is contemptible. Thus this christology creates more than an anthropology; it creates a lifestyle that disregards certain bodily considerations. The lack of any real union between the spiritual and physical in Christ leads to a spirituality in which it can be assumed that what I do with my body does not affect my soul. In other words, if the divine Christ did not really "touch" the man Jesus, then my inner spiritual being (the divine spark) does not really "touch" my body. Therefore I am free to participate in any physical activity I desire and compartmentalize that as separate from my religious beliefs. In some cases, this rejection of the body also leads to a rejection of marriage that is not at all ascetic. Ironically, like ascetic celibacy, it does reflect a certain eschatology, but unlike celibacy, it does not reflect a theology of waiting but rather a realized eschatology. This is not to say that all proponents of a hybrid christology must have lived a hedonistic lifestyle.[73] However, in general it does seem that (according to the heresiologists) there is a connection between the christology of these groups and their lifestyle via their anthropology.[74]

However, we must acknowledge the fact that we don't see the hedonism that the gnostics' contemporaries accused them of reflected in the primary documents that we have available to us, namely, the documents of the Nag Hammadi Library, which are mostly in the camp of Hybrid Gnosticism. Some scholars have claimed, therefore, that the accusations of hedonism in the early apologists and theologians are largely unfounded.[75] But while there are some passing references

---

[73]The Letter of Ptolemy does mention fasting, which makes it seem closer to mainstream Christianity on that issue. As Williams has pointed out, this does not imply an extreme asceticism (the kind we will expect to see in the true docetics), but it does speak against the traditional charges of "libertinism." See Williams, *Rethinking "Gnosticism,"* 141. The Exegesis of the Soul also can sound a bit ascetic in its condemnation of prostitution. However, it also allegorizes 1 Cor 6 in a way that could justify prostitution leaving the condemnation for a kind of spiritual prostitution or unfaithfulness. See The Exegesis of the Soul (in Robinson, *Nag Hammadi Library,* 194-95). This may be a way of speaking of the gnostic spiritual marriage as more enlightened than physical marriage, but in any case, these Ptolemaic documents are late and could represent further concession to the mainstream.

[74]For example, see Irenaeus of Lyons, *Against Heresies* 2.14; and Clement of Alexandria, *Stromateis* 3.5.

[75]Williams, *Rethinking "Gnosticism,"* 184-85. Interestingly, in an attempt to dismiss the witness of Irenaeus and the others as unfair and exaggerated slander, Williams does a good job of outlining the arguments against his own position.

to what appear to be ascetic practices, there is not enough there to disprove the witness of the theologians, which must be taken seriously, even if it is exaggerated.[76] After all, Irenaeus does not use the same "slander" against the proponents of a purely Docetic Gnosticism. For him, of course, they represent the other extreme, with the true church presenting the middle way. In reality, most of the documents of the Nag Hammadi Library do not speak about the lifestyle of their community at all, nor should we expect them to advertize their behavior if it might be considered antisocial or taboo.

Therefore the lack of evidence for a hedonistic lifestyle is not evidence against it. In addition, the Nag Hammadi documents are later redacted versions of what the earlier adherents may have believed, so it may be that (for books that were apparently collected by a more mainstream monastic community) any references to hedonism could have been filtered out in the collection process or edited out of the manuscripts. Just as likely, if Hybrid Gnosticism is already a syncretism of a syncretism, we should not look for a polarity of behavior, but more of a continuum, with some groups closer to the mainstream than others. In the end, the hedonism could have been one of the secrets reserved for members only, or even if it might have been an attraction to outsiders (one might even say a method of evangelism) it would not necessarily have been recorded in their theological documents. Thus, if the connection that I am making between christology and lifestyle is logical, it is not one that the gnostics openly acknowledged.

One final thought regarding the hedonism of Hybrid Gnosticism. It is possible that, to a certain extent, the lifestyle of the gnostics was not much different from the normal Roman lifestyle of the early empire. The charge of "libertinism" is made when it is compared to the expected lifestyle of Christians in an era of persecution. In other words, it could be that as the Hybrid Gnostics rejected the moral expectations of their more mainstream Christian counterparts and chose instead to live according to the values of Roman society, they

---

[76]See the interesting essay, "Afterword: The Modern Relevance of Gnosticism," in Robinson, *Nag Hammadi Library*, esp. 543-49.

appeared to be hedonistic when compared to the stricter communities—but were they really more hedonistic than non-Christian Romans? Perhaps only a little more so. If the charges of libertinism are exaggerated, it could simply be that they were living like pagans (which, of course, most of them had been). Roman religion rarely included proscriptions of behavior, and Roman morality was usually more about social decorum than sin, so that what went on behind closed doors was of no consequence as long as it stayed behind closed doors.[77] In any case, our present point is not to ask *how* hedonistic the Hybrid Gnostics were, but only to note that they were more hedonistic than the non-gnostic Christians and to explore the extent to which their lifestyle was enabled by a particular anthropology that in turn was created by their christology. This anthropology led them to disregard any concern for the treatment of their own bodies, but it apparently also led them to disregard the bodies of the poor by refusing to care for those less fortunate.[78]

Thus the traditional view of gnosticism, which sees the two radically different lifestyles of hedonism and asceticism as simply two options that flow equally from the same dualism, can be modified. It now appears much more likely that these two lifestyles are each the logical outcome of a different christology—two different starting points and their respective conclusions. Docetic christology, which denies any body of Christ, comes from a more radical dualism and leads to the denial of the human body in the form of asceticism. Hybrid Gnosticism on the other hand, which posits that Christ had a tangible body, comes from a lesser or compromised dualism but leads to a denigration of the body and consequently the free use (and abuse) of the human body.

---

[77]See Mike Aquilina and James L. Papandrea, *Seven Revolutions: How Christianity Changed the World and Can Change It Again* (New York: Random House/Image Books, 2015). As Williams points out, there are elements within gnosticism that sound like the Stoic virtue of apathy, as in a dispassionate indifference toward the things of the world. See Williams, *Rethinking "Gnosticism,"* 167. See the Apocryphon of John (in Robinson, *Nag Hammadi Library*, 115). There the document says, "From pleasure much wickedness arises." However, this is in the context of the heavenly realm. The point is that it may demonstrate a Stoic influence, which could have supported a disdain for the body.

[78]Ignatius of Antioch, *Letter to the Smyrnaeans* 6.2.

Until now, most studies have focused on the cosmology of the different gnostic systems, but here we have what I consider a useful category based specifically on christology, which in turn has implications for anthropology and even lifestyle. The insistence of the early apologists and theologians on a bodily resurrection of both Christ and believers demonstrates the relationship between christology and anthropology, but with very different implications from that within gnosticism. For the Hybrid Gnostics, the resurrection and ascension of the Christ exclude his body, ethereal though it may be. Therefore, part of the reason that gnostic christology was considered a threat to orthodoxy was that it implied an anthropology that separated the body from the essence of the person and left the human body unredeemed.

As a christology, Hybrid Gnosticism represents one of the four options in the early church in which proponents attempted to solve the problem of christology by making a sharp distinction between the divine Christ and the "man" Jesus of Nazareth. In the context of his polemic against them, Irenaeus would make it clear that we are not to separate Christ from Jesus, even to speak of the two natures.[79]

---

[79]Irenaeus of Lyons, *Against Heresies* 3.9.3; 3.11.7.

6

CHRIST AS WORD

Logos Christology

When it comes to Logos Christology, we are dealing with the understanding of Jesus Christ that won the day in the main-stream church of the second and third centuries and formed the basis for the christology that was declared dogma at the ecumenical councils and was codified in the Nicene Creed. In part, this under-standing of Christ won out because it was the view held by the ma-jority of Christians, or at least as far as we can tell, the majority of bishops and theologians.[1] But the reason the majority landed on this version of an explanation of the person of Christ is because they believed that this was the view most supported by the full witness of Scripture in both the Old and New Testaments.[2] In fact, the main-stream theologians argued that the proponents of the other views of Christ (the heretics) distorted the Scriptures, usually by picking and choosing among texts and latching onto the ones that, taken out of context, could support their teachings, while allegorizing away those that would not.[3] Therefore part of the definition of "orthodoxy" is

---

[1]Tertullian, *Prescription Against Heretics* 1.

[2]I would add that it is my belief that the process was guided by divine providence, and that—to put it boldly—this view of Christ won the day because it was correct. The *sensus fidelium*, guided by the Holy Spirit, inevitably led the church to the right understanding of Christ, since if the church had not maintained the understanding of Christ that God intended, it would have failed to be the church that Christ himself founded, and were that to happen, the gates of hell would indeed have prevailed against it (Mt 16:18).

[3]Tertullian, *Prescription Against Heretics* 9, 14, 17; Hippolytus, *Against Noetus* 3.

the refusal to ignore or explain away certain texts in favor of others. Orthodoxy is the acceptance of all of the prophetic and apostolic writings and asking, not which ones are true, but how they can all be true together.[4]

Since Logos Christology won out over the other christologies, we naturally have many more documents preserved from this camp. Furthermore, the documents that do exist are generally not anonymous—in other words, we know who wrote them, and so in our survey below we can take the documents together with their authors, the major proponents and developers of Logos Christology. However, it must be pointed out that, although we have a much clearer picture of the core beliefs of Logos Christology than we do of the other christologies, the beliefs as they are presented below are the result of a trajectory of development, or shall we say, increasing clarification, over time. This does not mean that the majority of the earliest Christians did not believe any particular aspect of Logos Christology—to say so would be an argument from silence. In fact, pre-Pauline quotations within the Pauline epistles are evidence that the majority of the earliest Christians did believe in a Logos Christology within the context of the doctrine of the Trinity.[5] However, this does mean that the beliefs that flowed from Scripture and from the Christian experience of worshiping the risen Christ took time to be clarified—often because they were not clarified until they were challenged by the alternative views we have surveyed so far.[6] In the next section, I will outline the core beliefs of Logos Christology as they were to be clarified by the middle of the third century. In the following section, the trajectory of development will become apparent as I outline the major proponents of Logos Christology and their particular contributions to the development of the church's understanding of Jesus Christ.

---

[4]See James L. Papandrea, *Reading the Early Church Fathers: From the Didache to Nicaea* (Mahwah, NJ: Paulist Press, 2012), 119-34.

[5]For an explanation of the pre-Pauline material and its relevance for christology and the doctrine of the Trinity, see James L. Papandrea, *Trinity 101: Father, Son, Holy Spirit* (Liguori, MO: Liguori, 2012), 27-50.

[6]Tertullian, *Prescription Against Heretics* 4, 30, 39. See also Papandrea, *Trinity 101*, 64-73.

Before we get to that, however, it is necessary to define what we mean by *Logos*. The term is a Greek word, often simply translated "word" but with a range of meanings that includes reason, rational principle, logic and even a divinely ordered structure. In Greek philosophical thought, it referred to the rational matrix of creation, the "soul" of the universe, sometimes personified as a quasi-divine entity. The apostle John, in his Gospel, combined the philosophical concept of the Logos with Hebrew wisdom tradition (such as Ps 33:6 and Prov 8:22-31) to speak about the divine nature of Jesus Christ, which preexisted his human nature.[7] In the incarnation, the divine Logos or *Word* of God came to be embodied in a human being (Jn 1:14).

In the aftermath of the destruction of the Jerusalem temple in the year 70 CE, both Jews and Christians (who were, at this time, still mostly Jews) struggled to understand how to worship God since the sacrifices were discontinued. As it turns out, both gravitated toward the Word of God, but in two different ways. Non-Christian Jews gravitated toward the Torah as the written Word of God. Christian Jews gravitated toward the person of Jesus Christ as the living Word of God. But unlike Jewish wisdom, or the philosophical world soul, the Christian Logos is not simply a personified concept that was really either an attribute of God or an impersonal force in the universe. He is an active subject—a person—relationally distinct from God the Father, yet also divine. He is not part of creation; he is Creator (Jn 1:2-3). According to John 1:1, "the Word was God" (the Word is divine), and yet "the Word was *with* God" (the Word is distinct from the Father; see also Jn 1:14, 18).

When examined in relation to the christologies we have surveyed so far, it becomes clear that Logos Christology is a kind of middle way among the five possible views (see the chart titled "Christology Continuum" at the end of this book). However, I do not mean a "middle way" in the sense of a compromise or a halfway point—rather, I mean that while the christologies on the extremes emphasized one nature of

---

[7]To some extent, John was following the lead of Philo of Alexandria, who also combined the philosophical concept of *logos* with the Hebrew concept of wisdom. For a more detailed treatment of the concept of Logos, see Papandrea, *Trinity 101*, 51-54.

Christ to the detriment of the other, Logos Christology refused to diminish either of Christ's two natures, affirming a "both-and" position.[8]

On one side, both forms of adoptionism denied or diminished the divinity of Jesus Christ by assuming that Jesus was a mere human who was either anointed by the Holy Spirit as a prophet (Spirit Adoptionism) or indwelt by an angelic spirit (Angel Adoptionism). In both cases the spiritual entity descends on a mere human, who is then elevated to a status of hero/redeemer (but only temporarily). This is a christology of ascent, since the man Jesus starts out in a lowly state, then is elevated by anointing and/or adoption by God the Father. This christology of ascent results in the separation of the man Jesus from "the Christ," who is the anointing spiritual entity, either the Holy Spirit (Spirit Adoptionism) or a created angel (Angel Adoptionism).

On the other side, both forms of gnosticism diminish the humanity of Jesus Christ by assuming that Jesus' body is either an illusion (docetism/Docetic Gnosticism) or a less-than-human vessel (Hybrid Gnosticism). Here "the Christ" may be divine (or more precisely quasi-divine, since this entity is not necessarily eternal), but there is no human element to the Savior, and therefore he did not represent humanity on the cross. With regard to the divinity, the gnostics accepted the concept of degrees of divinity and also believed that the gods could procreate, which meant that some of the gods had a beginning to their existence—they were born into existence from nonexistence. This effectively blurred the line between what we would consider Creator and created beings, since for the gnostics many of their gods could be both. This is not a christology of ascent, but neither is it a christology of descent, since the divine (or quasi-divine) spiritual entity never really makes contact with humanity, let alone the material world.

Logos Christology, as a middle way between these alternatives, refuses to allow either of Jesus Christ's two natures to be diminished. Logos Christology embraces a full divinity that is preexistent and a true humanity with a real human body. This is a christology of descent,

---

[8]For more on orthodoxy as the middle way between alternatives on the extremes, see Papandrea, *Reading the Early Church Fathers*, 139-47, and *Trinity 101*, 64-88.

because the divine Logos starts out in the divine realm as equal to the Father and descends to humanity to take on our human condition (Phil 2:6-8). Furthermore, Logos Christology refuses to separate Jesus from "the Christ" as though they are two separate entities, but rather considers the whole incarnate Jesus Christ as one person.[9]

THE CORE OF LOGOS CHRISTOLOGY

The experience of the first disciples meeting the risen Christ, and the worship of Christ in the earliest Christian churches, led the majority of the church to understand the one God as manifest in three entities (eventually called *persons*), who are distinct enough that they are not simply three names for the one God nor descriptions of three kinds of divine activity; yet they are unified enough that they are not three Gods. In describing God, Justin Martyr said that the Father has the first place, the Son takes the second place and the Spirit takes the third place.[10] The Greek fathers of the second century referred to God as the divine *Triad*. In the third century, the Latin term *Trinity* was coined.

The one who takes the second place—the one who would come to be called the second person of the Trinity—is the Logos. He is the divine nature incarnate in Jesus Christ. He existed before his incarnation, in fact before creation, and was manifest and visible in certain Old Testament theophanies, including appearances of the "Angel of the Lord."[11] At his incarnation (his conception at the annunciation), the Logos acquired a human nature, which was created in the womb of Mary. It would later be clarified that the whole person of Jesus Christ, both natures of divinity and humanity, was born into the world from the womb of Mary, so that it is appropriate to call her the Mother of God.[12]

---

[9]Irenaeus of Lyons, *Against Heresies* 3.9.3; 3.11.7.

[10]Justin Martyr, *1 Apology* 13, 60.

[11]The belief that the Logos is *eternally* preexistent is not necessarily evident in the prologue to John. This will be discussed below. However, it is not the case that the fourth Gospel is the first time we see the preexistence of the Logos. The pre-Pauline hymn in Phil 2 is evidence of the early belief in preexistence. See Papandrea, *Trinity 101*, 10-63. On the preexistent Logos in the Old Testament, see James L. Papandrea, *Novatian of Rome and Culmination of Pre-Nicene Orthodoxy*, Princeton Theological Monograph 175 (Eugene, OR: Pickwick, 2011), 7-8.

[12]For more detail on this point, see Papandrea, *Reading the Early Church Fathers*, 210-19.

Therefore Jesus Christ is one person who is both human and divine. There is no separation of Jesus from "the Christ" as if they were two entities. Irenaeus of Lyons explained that it is never appropriate to name the human nature "Jesus" and the divine nature "Christ" since that kind of separation is something the gnostics do.[13] However, Logos Christology does make a distinction (not a separation) between the divine and human natures of Christ in order to safeguard the immutability and impassibility of the divine by reserving the suffering of Christ to the human nature alone. This is a subtle, but important, difference between Logos Christology and the other christologies. Perhaps in all cases the goal is to preserve the immutability of the divine. The gnostics do it by denying any contact of the divine with the material world. The adoptionists do it by denying that the one who suffered and died was really divine. Logos Christology does it by maintaining that the human nature of Jesus Christ suffered while the divine nature did not. Thus the unity of the person is preserved as well as the immutability of the divine. We will explore why this is important in the conclusion below. Also preserved is the uniqueness of Jesus Christ among humanity, for while he is truly one of us, he is unique among us.

Logos Christology, therefore, is properly called an incarnation—the embodiment of the divine—as opposed to an indwelling/inhabitation (as in Angel Adoptionism or Hybrid Gnosticism) or an anointing (as in Spirit Adoptionism). In the other christologies (with the exception of Docetic Gnosticism, which has no union with a tangible element at all), the union of the human with the spiritual entity is temporary. Logos Christology, on the other hand, is an incarnation that results in a permanent and unbreakable union of the divine nature with the human. Once incarnate, the two natures cannot be separated, though a certain distinction remains, preserving the integrity of each nature. As the theologian Tertullian put it, the unborn was united with the born in the one person of Jesus Christ.[14] This results in a real historical person who is fully human (that is, human as we are human, Heb 4:15) and also

---

[13]Irenaeus of Lyons, *Against Heresies* 3.9.3; 3.11.7.
[14]Tertullian, *On the Flesh of Christ* 5.

fully divine (that is, not quasi-divine, but divine as God the Father is divine, Phil 2:6). It also results in a Savior who is not abandoned by the spiritual entity at any point, not even at the cross. And Jesus Christ never ceases to be fully human, even after his ascension.

Finally, unlike the christologies on both sides, Logos Christology affirms that the resurrection of Jesus Christ was not an illusion or a metaphor but a real bodily resurrection. The mainstream church came to believe that because he was willing to take on a human body, this was an implicit affirmation of the goodness of the body, and that meant that the human body would be redeemed. It is not, as some philosophers taught, a shell to be discarded. It is part of the whole human being. And as such, loving one's neighbor meant more than imparting spiritual wisdom; it also meant feeding the hungry and giving hospitality to the homeless (Mt 25:31-46).

The Major Proponents and Their Primary Documents

Each of the important writers I will survey below was responding to what they perceived as the most pressing problems of the church in their day. In the second century, the problem of persecution led the apologists, such as Justin Martyr, to write a justification of the faith for a pagan audience. In these apologies, Christian philosophers were attempting to explain their beliefs to outsiders. Later, beginning with Irenaeus, the problem of heresy turned the attention of the early theologians to an internal audience, warning the faithful of the dangers of incorrect belief. None of these writers were attempting to create a systematic theology—in fact they were all responding to the christologies we have looked at so far in the previous chapters. However, their convictions are based on the assumption that Logos Christology is the more original, and more biblical, understanding of the person of Jesus Christ. At no time do these authors imply or allow that what they are teaching is new.[15] The assumption is always that the doctrines they advocate reflect the long-standing (traditional) beliefs of the majority of Christians.

---

[15]Tertullian, *Prescription Against Heretics* 29, 31.

Ignatius of Antioch (ca. 50–110 CE). According to early Christian historians, Ignatius was a disciple of the apostle John. Just after the turn of the century, the bishop of Antioch in Syria was arrested as part of a general persecution of church leaders during the reign of the emperor Trajan.[16] Like the apostle Paul, he must have played the Roman citizenship card, and so he was sent to Rome under guard for trial and execution. Also like Paul, he was allowed to meet with fellow Christians along the way and wrote (or dictated) several letters that are still available.[17] In these letters, Ignatius affirms both natures of Jesus Christ against those who would deny or diminish either one. Apparently Ignatius was most concerned about a fringe element teaching a docetic christology (cf. 1 Jn 4:1-3), and so he emphasized that the human birth of Christ, and the suffering of his passion, prove his true humanity.[18] However, he also affirmed the true divinity of Christ against adoptionist christology, referring to Jesus Christ as "God" and clarifying that the Logos was not only preexistent but eternally so.[19] This is important because the prologue to the fourth Gospel could be interpreted as though the Logos were preexistent (existed before and at creation) but not eternal. In fact, later adoptionists would say precisely this—that the Logos was the first created being, and therefore was present at the creation of the rest of the universe, but was not eternal. Here Ignatius rules out that interpretation in favor of the full divinity—and eternity—of the Logos.

The adoptionists were arguing that because Jesus obviously changed throughout his life and suffered on the cross, his mutability and passibility

---

[16]See the letter of Pliny the Younger to Trajan, *Epistle* 10, and Trajan's reply. This correspondence took place at about the same time that Ignatius's letters were written. On the context of persecution, see Papandrea, *Novatian of Rome*, 47-53; and Papandrea, *Reading the Early Church Fathers*, 10-17, 156-60.

[17]There is a long history of scholarship on the authenticity of the letters, and in fact there are several versions of the authentic letters and several spurious letters to which Ignatius's name is attached. It is my assumption that the authentic letters are the seven letters to the Ephesians, Magnesians, Trallians, Romans, Philadelphians, Smyrnaeans and to Polycarp, bishop of Smyrna. For each of these letters, the middle recension is the one most likely to be authentic.

[18]Ignatius of Antioch, *Letter to the Ephesians* 7.7; 18.2; 19.1; *Letter to the Magnesians* 8.1, 11; *Letter to the Trallians* 9.1-2; 10.1; *Letter to the Smyrnaeans* 1.1-2; 2.1; 4.2; 5.2.

[19]Ignatius of Antioch, *Letter to the Ephesians* 7.2; *Letter to the Magnesians* 8.1; *Letter to the Philadelphians* 6.1.

ruled out his divinity. In other words, because he suffered, he could not be divine. On the other side, the docetics argued that the Christ spirit did not really make contact with humanity, and some went so far as to say that Jesus, as a man, never really existed. In other words, because he was divine (or quasi-divine), he could not really be human, let alone suffer. Against both of these positions Ignatius speaks for the mainstream church, offering the middle way and affirming both natures. The human nature, the Son of Man/Son of Mary, could grow, suffer and die, while the divine nature, the Son of God, remained immutable and impassible.[20] This practice of labeling the human nature as the Son of Man (or Son of David, or Son of Mary) and the divine nature as the Son of God would not last, as it would come to be recognized later that both labels should refer to the whole person of Christ. However, Ignatius's contribution to the clarification of Logos Christology is important because he bridges the distance from the New Testament to the apologists, affirming what the apostles believed—that Jesus Christ is one person who is truly human and fully divine. And this full divinity means that he must also be eternal.

Justin Martyr (ca. 112–165 CE). Justin was born at about the time Ignatius was executed. He came from the eastern empire but settled in Rome and set up shop as a teacher of philosophy. He had explored all of the philosophical options available in the Roman Empire of his day and found Christianity to be the most convincing. Justin would later admit that part of what led to his conversion to the church was witnessing the bravery of the martyrs.[21] He would eventually join their ranks when the pagan philosophers of Rome betrayed him to the authorities.

During his time in Rome, Justin taught Christianity as a philosophy. He was a lay teacher who gathered disciples and taught out of his apartment above a public bathhouse. There the faithful and the curious would gather to hear Justin explain the faith. During the reign of the emperor Antoninus Pius, the persecution of Christians led

---

[20]Ignatius of Antioch, *Letter to the Ephesians* 7.2; 18.2; 20.2; *Letter to the Smyrnaeans* 1.1; *Letter to Polycarp* 3.2.
[21]Justin Martyr, *2 Apology* 12.

Justin to write an open letter to the emperor, a letter that we know of as his *First Apology* (*1 Apology*). His *Second Apology* (*2 Apology*) was addressed to the next emperor, Marcus Aurelius. In these writings, and in a document written for a Jewish audience called the *Dialogue with Trypho*, Justin attempted to convince non-Christians that Christianity was a reasonable belief system and that Christians should not be persecuted. And because he was writing to a pagan philosophical audience, the concept of the Logos seemed the perfect way to present Jesus Christ in a positive light.

Justin was fascinated with the way the apostles described the life and ministry of Jesus Christ as a fulfillment of Old Testament prophecy, and he further connected Christ to the Old Testament by pointing out that since the Logos is preexistent, he was around during the time of the patriarchs and prophets. In fact, the preincarnate Jesus can be seen in the Old Testament if one knows where to look. Since we read in Exodus 33:20 that no one can see the face of God and live to tell about it (see also 1 Tim 6:16), and since there were times in the Old Testament when people did claim to have seen God, Justin reasoned that the Exodus passage must be interpreted to mean that no one can see *the Father* and live—but one could see the Son. After all, in his incarnation, he was both visible and tangible, and so that ability to be seen must be a personal privilege of the second person of the Trinity, available to him even before his incarnation. This meant that an epiphany of the divine in the Old Testament (such as in Gen 18) must actually be an appearance of the preincarnate Logos.[22] In fact, since the Logos is the *Word* of God, whenever God seems to be speaking, it is actually the voice of the Logos that is heard—including in Moses' burning bush.[23]

Justin seems heavily influenced by the Johannine documents, as we

---

[22]Justin Martyr, *1 Apology* 63. See also *Dialogue with Trypho* 56-60; 127.1-2. Irenaeus follows Justin in this line of reasoning; see, e.g., Irenaeus of Lyons, *Demonstration of the Apostolic Preaching* 32. For more on the appearances of the second person of the Trinity in the Old Testament, see Papandrea, *Trinity 101*, 10-17; and Papandrea, *Novatian of Rome*, 7-8, 21, 42-43, 97, 102-3.

[23]Justin Martyr, *1 Apology* 62-63. Not all of the early church fathers agreed on this point. They would all agree that God spoke to humanity with the voice of the Logos, but there was no consensus on exactly when it was the Logos speaking (most often when a voice was heard) versus the Holy Spirit (e.g., in inspiring the prophets).

should expect, and he follows those writings in demonstrating a balance of unity and distinction within the Trinity. In terms of unity, the Logos is one divinity with the Father.[24] This is, of course, necessary to maintain a monotheistic God. To say otherwise would imply three Gods. But what is important is that Justin is offhandedly expressing an already existing belief that would set the stage for the early theologians Irenaeus and Tertullian to articulate the doctrine of *consubstantiality*—that the Father and the Son (and indeed the Holy Spirit) are of one divine substance. This also leads Justin to a doctrine that goes hand in hand with consubstantiality, that of *inseparable operation*. This is the conviction that all three persons of the Trinity are united in all divine activity, and although Justin does not name it or express it in the way it will be expressed later, he certainly understood the importance of seeing all three persons of the Trinity as one divine power and one united activity.[25]

In terms of the distinction of persons in the Trinity, Justin clarifies that although the Father and Son are *one* (Jn 10:30), they are not *one and the same* (Jn 14:28).[26] The distinction between them is demonstrated by the fact that there is an order, in fact a hierarchy, within the Trinity in which the Father has a certain precedence over the Son and the Son over the Spirit.[27] Specifically, the Son is the Father's *Angel*, not in the sense of a created being, but in the sense of the literal meaning of the Greek word *angelos*, meaning "messenger" or "agent," and so the hierarchy is one of Sender and Messenger.[28] When it comes to creation, the Son is the agent of creation—no less Creator than the Father, and yet only the Father is the First Cause and Ultimate Source of creation. This does not diminish the unity of the three persons, but it does safeguard the distinction between them, and for Justin and those after him, it prevents trinitarian theology from falling into a kind of

---

[24]Justin Martyr, *1 Apology* 6; 33. See also *Dialogue with Trypho* 61; 128.

[25]Justin Martyr, *Dialogue with Trypho* 56. Note that Ignatius hints at inseparable operation as well (Ignatius of Antioch, *Letter to the Magnesians* 7).

[26]Justin Martyr, *Dialogue with Trypho* 56; 62; 128-29.

[27]Justin Martyr, *1 Apology* 13; 60.

[28]Justin Martyr, *1 Apology* 12; 63. Note that assuming the Old Testament appearances of the "Angel of the Lord" were the preincarnate Logos fits well into this framework (see Mt 21:33-41; Mk 12:1-12; Lk 20:9-18).

functionalism (modalism) that sees the three persons of the Trinity as three different activities of God or reduces them to three names for a single divine person.[29]

Irenaeus of Lyons (ca. 125-202 CE). According to tradition, Irenaeus was from Smyrna in Asia Minor and was sent from there by Bishop Polycarp to be a missionary and assist the bishop of Lyons in Gaul. Not long after his arrival, however, the bishop of Lyons was martyred and Irenaeus was elected his successor. Irenaeus wrote two works that are still extant, a longer work, *Against Heresies* (written mostly against gnosticism), and a shorter work, *Demonstration* [or *Proof*] *of the Apostolic Preaching*. His most important contribution to Logos Christology is probably the fact that he took Justin's teaching on the one divinity of the Father and the Son to its logical conclusion. He wrote that the Father and Son are of one *essence*, clarifying that the unity of the persons of the Trinity is an ontological unity and that ultimately God is one because there is only one divinity or divine essence.[30] Here the doctrine of *consubstantiality* is explicitly expressed, refuting both the gnostic denial that the God of the Old Testament is the same as the one whom Jesus called Father as well as the adoptionist denial of the divinity of Jesus Christ.[31]

It was also important to Irenaeus to expand on Justin's concept of the preincarnate Logos as the Angel of the Father. Since gnostics tended to reject the Old Testament, Irenaeus argued for its value by showing how Jesus Christ appeared there.[32] However, it is the incarnation that was the lynchpin of his argument against the gnostics, and indeed he believed it was the center of all of human history. While the gnostics denied that Christ took on true humanity (their dualism did not allow

---

[29]Justin's language on this point is neither precise nor well developed, and it would not be until later writers that the church would have a clearly defined distinction between the Son and the Spirit. In fact, it is typical of the apologists to blur the distinction between the preincarnate Logos and the Holy Spirit. For example, see Justin Martyr, *1 Apology* 13; 60; *Dialogue with Trypho* 61. See also Ignatius of Antioch, *Letter to the Ephesians* 7.2. In spite of the lack of a developed pneumatology, this does demonstrate an original belief in the divinity of the Holy Spirit.

[30]Irenaeus of Lyons, *Demonstration of the Apostolic Preaching* 47.

[31]Irenaeus of Lyons, *Against Heresies* 2.31.1; 4.32.1.

[32]Irenaeus of Lyons, *Against Heresies* 1.19.2; 3.6.1; 4.10.1.

the "mingling" of the spiritual with the material), Irenaeus affirmed that the Logos had to become human in order to save humanity.[33] This is an early expression of something that would become axiomatic for the church: *what is not assumed is not redeemed.* In other words, it is our humanity that is burdened by sin, and it is our humanity that needs redemption; therefore it could only be by taking on our humanity that the Savior can save us. In fact, Irenaeus argued that if Christ were not really human, but only appeared to be human as the docetics argued, then he is a deceiver, and his teachings should not be trusted.[34]

Irenaeus could be considered the pioneer of another important axiom of orthodoxy, specifically, that the one who is begotten must be of the same ontological essence as the one who begets.[35] To use an oversimplified analogy, dogs beget puppies and not kittens because a dog can only produce another dog. When the principle is applied to the Trinity, the point is that the Father, who is God, can only beget a Son who is also God. The Son must be a chip off the old divine block—in other words, of the same divine essence as the Father. This becomes Irenaeus's logical proof for the doctrine of consubstantiality as well as inseparable operation.

Finally, Irenaeus (writing to a Christian audience) pointed out the implications of christology for salvation. The christ of the adoptionists could not save because such a christ would not be the embodiment of the divine and would lack the element of divine intervention.[36] A docetic or gnostic christ could not save because such a christ did not take on our situation by assuming real humanity.[37] Only a Savior who is both divine and human could be the Savior of humanity. In other words, to believe in the wrong kind of savior is to believe in no savior at all. Almost one thousand years later, Anselm of Canterbury would use this concept as the basis for his famous treatise on the incarnation and atonement, *Cur Deus Homo?* (*Why the God-Man?*).[38]

---

[33]Irenaeus of Lyons, *Against Heresies* 2.22.4.

[34]Irenaeus of Lyons, *Against Heresies* 3.18.7.

[35]Irenaeus of Lyons, *Against Heresies* 2.17.3-7. The principle is based on the assumption of divine simplicity.

[36]Irenaeus of Lyons, *Against Heresies* 3.20.3; 4.6.7; 4.33.4.

[37]Irenaeus of Lyons, *Against Heresies* 4.6.7; 5.14.3.

[38]See Papandrea, *Reading the Early Church Fathers*, 219-25.

Tertullian (ca. 145–225 CE). There is some debate about whether Tertullian was ever ordained, but it seems that by the time he wrote his major theological works he was writing as a lay teacher. While the apologists had used the Greek word *triados* (Triad) for God, it was Tertullian who gave us the Latin *trinitas*, or "Trinity." In fact, Tertullian is the first theologian to write in Latin, and marks the beginning of the Western church's shift away from Greek as its official language. Nevertheless, from his home in Carthage, North Africa, he was a faithful student of the writings of Irenaeus. He accepted Irenaeus's maxim that the one who is begotten must be of the same essence as the one who begets.[39] He translated Irenaeus's "one essence" into its Latin equivalent, "one substance," and gave us a way to speak of God as *one divine substance, three persons.*

Tertullian wrote many documents, but a few are most important for our purposes. In *Against Marcion* and *On the Flesh of Christ,* he refutes docetic and gnostic christologies by demonstrating the reality of Christ's humanity.[40] In fact, Tertullian affirmed that the union of humanity with the divine Logos was not temporary and that Jesus Christ retains his full humanity, even after the ascension.[41] On the other hand, he affirmed the full divinity of Christ as well, and it is in the document *Against Praxeas* that he explains consubstantiality as well as defines what would become standard terminology for the Trinity in the West.[42] The Father, Son and Holy Spirit are described as three *persons,* yet the singular divinity is maintained by emphasizing that the three persons are one *substance* (that substance being divinity itself).[43] The word *person* describes the

---

[39]Tertullian, *On the Flesh of Christ* 18; *Against Praxeas* 8.
[40]Tertullian, *On the Flesh of Christ* 16.
[41]Ibid.
[42]Tertullian, *On the Flesh of Christ* 5; *Against Praxeas* 25.
[43]In trinitarian terminology, *persons* is not the equivalent of "people," so it would not be accurate to describe the Father, Son and Holy Spirit as three divine people. This would imply too much distinction—to the point of separation—and not enough unity in the Trinity. In this sense, the word *persons* is a technical term meant to convey the distinction between Father, Son and Holy Spirit (they are not one person with three names), yet maintain the unity (they are still one in essence/substance and in power/activity). Note that the *substance* of the Trinity is not a tangible substance, but it is the very essence of divinity. See Tertullian, *Against Praxeas* 31.1.

triplicity ("threeness") of God, while the term *substance* describes the unity (oneness).[44]

Tertullian expanded on the doctrine of inseparable operation and also the concept of a hierarchy in the Trinity.[45] These two ideas, taken together, might appear to be a paradox, but that is precisely the point. Adoptionists and gnostics alike (each for their own reasons) would deny inseparable operation and expand the hierarchical distinction between the Father and the Son to the point of making it a separation. For the adoptionists, this took the Son out of the divine realm. For the gnostics, it made him another god. For Irenaeus, and especially for Tertullian, the doctrine of inseparable operation and the concept of a hierarchy in the Trinity balance each other out and actually solve the problem of how to maintain that Jesus Christ is God without compromising monotheism.[46]

Like Irenaeus, Tertullian emphasized the importance of the incarnation in the story of human history and salvation. Because of the incarnation, the divine Logos took on a human nature, and so the second person of the Trinity is one person with two substances (natures), divinity and humanity.[47] And it must be that way—the Logos must have become truly human in order to be the savior of humanity, since *what is not assumed is not redeemed.*[48]

Finally, Tertullian described the union of the divine and human in the person of Jesus Christ in ways that anticipated the conclusions of later christological debates (the hypostatic union). Just as the relationship of persons in the Trinity is a balance of unity and distinction, so in the person of Christ the union of divine and human is a balance of unity and distinction. The two natures retain their integrity (which is required for the divine nature to remain immutable), and yet the two natures are inseparably united in one person.[49]

---

[44]See also Tertullian, *Apology* 21.12.

[45]Tertullian, *On the Flesh of Christ* 14.

[46]See Papandrea, *Trinity 101*, 64-82.

[47]Tertullian, *On the Flesh of Christ* 4-5; 17; *Against Praxeas* 7; 27; *Against Marcion* 20. The normal term for the two aspects of Christ's person, divinity and humanity, is "natures"; however, in this sense it is synonymous with *essences* or *substances*. The divine nature/substance of Jesus Christ is the same divine substance as the singular substance of the Trinity.

[48]Tertullian, *On the Flesh of Christ* 4; 10.

[49]Tertullian, *On the Flesh of Christ* 13; 17; 19; *Against Praxeas* 27.

Novatian (ca. 200–258 CE). With Novatian, in the middle of the third century, we are moving toward the ecumenical councils of the fourth century. In fact, it could be said that Novatian does not exhibit Logos Christology but moves beyond it to lay the foundation for Nicene theology.[50] Nevertheless, he is included here as the capstone of early mainstream (orthodox) christology. Novatian rounds out Logos Christology by taking the very aspects we have been exploring from the apologists Irenaeus and Tertullian and pushing them to their logical conclusions.

In one important case, he had to correct a misunderstanding of those who came before him. Specifically, all of the apologists and theologians before Novatian had assumed that the "begetting" (or generation) of the Son from the Father was an *event* that *took place* at *some point* in eternity before creation.[51] In other words, even though they believed that the Logos was eternally preexistent, their descriptions of his preexistence could be interpreted as though he was not eternally distinct from the Father and that he originally existed as no more than a thought in the Father's mind until such point at which he was "emitted" like a "word" from the Father's "mouth." The problem with this is that it implied a change in the Logos, compromising divine immutability and perhaps even implying that God was not always a Trinity. Novatian recognized that for the Trinity to be eternally a Trinity, and for the Father to be always a Father, it was required that the second person of the Trinity be not only eternal but also an eternally distinct divine person. Therefore the generation of the Son could not be an event that took place at some point (before which he was not yet begotten); rather the generation of the Son must be an eternal state of being, in which both Father and Son were in relationship—the Father as source of generation, the Son as the one who was generated. Thus Novatian was the first theologian to comprehend the concept of *eternal generation*.[52] This concept goes hand in hand with the doctrines we have already seen, specifically consubstantiality and inseparable operation.

---

[50]See Papandrea, *Novatian of Rome.*
[51]Ibid., 12-15, 33-34.
[52]Ibid., 85-92.

Summary and Implications

Logos Christology was the view of the majority of the church, and yet it was only clarified after the alternative christologies presented themselves in response. Therefore, it must be made clear that it is incorrect to presume that orthodoxy did not exist until the church's christology was settled at the ecumenical councils. The truth is, there is an orthodoxy in every generation of the church's existence, and this is precisely because the mainstream writers were arguing in opposition to what they considered heresy. Certainly Irenaeus had a sense of orthodoxy when he wrote *Against Heresies*. Therefore it is not necessary to speak of a "proto-orthodoxy," or indeed to put the word *orthodoxy* in quotation marks when dealing with the earliest centuries of the church. Each generation's orthodoxy is based on the foundation of the orthodoxy of the previous generation, going back to the apostles and their writings, which became our Scriptures. Therefore heresy does not precede orthodoxy, although in some ways it does precede the *clarification* of orthodoxy.

Logos Christology is the mainstream church's place of balance—a middle way between the extremes of adoptionism on one side and gnosticism on the other. Both extremes denied the incarnation, turning it into either an anointing or an indwelling or reducing it to a mere illusion.[53] In all of these scenarios, there is no real embodiment of the divine and hence no real contact with humanity. Furthermore, it is erroneous to speak of mainstream (orthodox) christology— especially New Testament christology—as either high or low christology. To be high or low is to be heretical. Gnosticism is a high christology, emphasizing the divinity but diminishing the humanity. Adoptionism is a low christology, emphasizing the humanity but denying the divinity. Logos Christology is neither high nor low precisely because it embraces the paradox of Jesus Christ's two natures and presents a balanced understanding of his person.

Just as there is a balance of unity and distinction between the three persons of the Trinity, so also there is a balance of unity and distinction

---

[53]Irenaeus of Lyons, *Against Heresies* 3.11.3; 3.20.4; 5.19.2.

between the two natures of the second person. He is fully divine (divine as the Father is, and not quasi-divine), and he is truly human (human as we are, yet without sin).[54] These two natures are united in a way that maintains the integrity of each (preserving the immutability and impassibility of the divine), yet also in such a way that they are inseparable. By the time of Tertullian and Novatian, their descriptions of the union of the two natures within the one person of Christ anticipates the definition of the *hypostatic union* of the ecumenical councils. It is therefore incorrect to label the human nature "Jesus" and the divine nature "Christ," since this would compromise the unity of his person.[55] In fact, it is exactly this union of divine and human in the person of Christ that makes the union of humanity with God possible, and to diminish this union with a separation of "Jesus" and "Christ" is to put at risk our very salvation. Therefore contemporary attempts to distinguish between "the Jesus of history" and "the Christ of faith" are ultimately spiritually impotent.

As Logos Christology opposed the forms of adoptionism and gnosticism that we have surveyed in the chapters above, it affirmed both natures of Christ. Against adoptionism, the Logos is eternally generated from the Father, which means that he is coeternal and consubstantial with the Father.[56] He is the Son of the Father (who is one and the same as the God of the Old Testament), and he is the Agent of Creation.[57] Thus it is appropriate to worship him, and doing so does not compromise monotheism. The Logos could also be seen making preincarnation appearances to humanity in the theophanies of the Old Testament.

Against gnosticism, the Logos was incarnate as a human being who was truly one of us. His human nature grew, suffered and died, while

---

[54]It is not correct to say that if Jesus Christ were fully human he would have sinned. Sin is not part of humanity, but is in fact less than fully human. To sin is to fall short of human potential. Jesus Christ, as sinless, is arguably more fully human than the rest of us, since we regularly compromise our humanity through sin.

[55]Irenaeus of Lyons, *Against Heresies* 3.9.3; 3.11.7.

[56]In addition to the primary sources listed above, see also Hippolytus, *Refutation of All Heresies* 10.28-29; *Against Noetus* 11.

[57]As the second person of the Trinity, the Son is God, and because of the doctrine of inseparable operation, it is legitimate to call Jesus Christ Creator. However, technically speaking, only the Father is the Ultimate Source of creation, the First Cause of all existence.

his divine nature remained immutable and impassible. However, his divine nature participated in the incarnation to such an extent that it is legitimate to say that the whole person of Jesus Christ, divine and human, was born into the world through the womb of Mary and was made visible and tangible through his human body. To use the biblical language, the Word *became* human, and the early Logos theologians argued that it must be this way for salvation to be possible, since what is not assumed is not redeemed.

Furthermore, salvation requires both natures, since the Logos theologians would argue that salvation could not be accomplished without both divine intervention and human representation. Adoptionism has the human element but lacks divine intervention. The adoptionist Jesus is reduced to one who sets a good example, resulting in a salvation by works. Gnosticism could be said to have a divine element but lacks the human representation, since the gnostic Christ is not really one of us. This results in a salvation by enlightenment (knowledge/gnosis), but only for the special few. Logos Christology has both aspects of salvation—the divine nature providing the divine intervention and the human nature providing the human representation.[58]

The incarnation is therefore best described as a descent, since Jesus Christ is God who became human. He is not a human who was elevated to hero status, nor was he a god who deceived humanity by pretending to be human. He is the second person of the Trinity, whose works are inseparable from the Trinity (inseparable operation). Thus while he is truly human, he is unique among humanity. Ironically, both extreme alternatives deny the uniqueness of Jesus Christ. Adoptionism calls him a mere human, like the rest of us, and gnosticism preaches that we are gods as he is. Logos Christology preserves his uniqueness as the Son of God while affirming that he is truly one of us.

Logos Christology also affirms a real bodily resurrection of Jesus Christ against the alternative christologies, all of which would have denied a bodily resurrection. Adoptionists, for the most part, probably considered the resurrection a metaphor for eternal life, while the

---

[58]See Papandrea, *Reading the Early Church Fathers*, 219-25.

gnostics considered the idea of a resurrection unnecessary for someone who was never really able to die. But for the Logos theologians, the resurrection of Christ is important because it further affirms the goodness and value of the human body, and it foreshadows our own resurrection and makes it possible.

One last thing deserves mentioning. Since Logos Christology affirms the true humanity of Jesus Christ—in fact that the divine Logos was willing to descend to take on our human nature with a real human body—this means that the human body is a good and necessary part of our humanity. It is not a shell to be discarded, as the philosophers taught, and it is not evil, as the gnostics taught. It is to be respected as a creation of God, and as such it is to be valued, especially when we see the human body of our neighbors suffering. Therefore the response of the mainstream church to the suffering of fellow human beings was to see Christ in them and to care for them. In terms of lifestyle, although some Christians chose a life of asceticism, most Christians looked for a balanced approach to their bodies, neither indulging them nor punishing them.

7

WHAT, THEN, IS ORTHODOXY?

As I noted at the start of this examination of early christology, the five views of Christ I have presented here are neater, cleaner and more well-defined than they would have been in "real life" in the second century. Even the theologians of the time, such as Irenaeus, sometimes conflated or mislabeled certain groups, and the heresiologists who came later did so on an even greater scale. In order to understand the different interpretations of the person of Christ, we necessarily have to boil them down to essentials and to describe them as factions in order to compare them to each other. And although these factions did exist, they did not necessarily have universal agreement or even internal consensus on many of the points of belief attributed to them.

Even where we have primary-source documents from these factions, the documents themselves are not internally consistent (often due to layers of tradition added over years of editing, perhaps sometimes to make concessions to the mainstream) and sometimes they are so convoluted that they defy understanding. It may have been the case that, for the average believer in the early church—especially in the larger cities—the boundaries between the factions could seem fluid and the differences in belief too small to matter, and it could probably be very confusing for some people to know which teachers they should believe, which leaders they should follow and even to which congregation they should belong.

This is not to say that everyone was confused or that every option seemed as good as the others at the time. In fact the bishops constantly preached and the theologians constantly wrote to protect their people from heresy. Because they believed that souls were at stake, they could not simply let everyone believe whatever they wanted to. To believe the wrong things about Christ was to believe in the wrong christ, and that christ (being nonexistent) could not save.

WHY DID LOGOS CHRISTOLOGY WIN?

There are two main reasons why Logos Christology won out over the other options: apostolic succession and Logos Christology's middle-way approach.

Apostolic succession. The apostles were, in effect, the first bishops, each of whom came to assume a regional authority over multiple congregations. In the cities where they had influence, they appointed their successors, who became the next generation of bishops. In those cities without direct apostolic oversight, the first bishops were probably elected by a council of priests.[1] In every subsequent generation, the bishops of each city could claim succession going back to the first generation of bishops and, through the apostles, to Jesus himself.[2] In this way the bishops held authority over the doctrine of the church and over what was being taught to the people.

Therefore, in every generation of the church, it must have been clear to most Christians who the "mainstream" church was—that is, which congregations were in communion with the bishops in succession from the apostles—and these congregations would certainly have represented the majority of people calling themselves Christian. Having said this, it is not necessarily the case that the heretics confined themselves to specific congregations led by known heretical leaders. In many places, especially in the larger cities, there must have been a range of beliefs within every group and multiple teachers drawing the attention of the faithful. Even Justin Martyr apparently operated as a

---

[1]James L. Papandrea, *Reading the Early Church Fathers: From the Didache to Nicaea* (Mahwah, NJ: Paulist Press, 2012), 47-54.
[2]Ibid., 21-22.

lay teacher/philosopher in Rome without being part of the hierarchy. Undoubtedly some of the leaders of heretical movements started out this way and gathered followers who nevertheless continued worshiping with their house church in communion with their bishop. Other heresies were started or promoted by priests who deviated from the authorized teachings of their bishops, or even by bishops who deviated from the authorized teachings of their predecessors.

Still, there was a universal church of the apostles, and it was to be found in the congregations that were in communion with the bishops, who were in turn in communion with their predecessors through apostolic succession. As history—or providence—would have it, it was Logos Christology that was the christology of the mainstream church and its bishops.[3] Logos Christology was the interpretation of the person of Christ that was considered by the majority of bishops to be consistent with the teachings of the apostles, especially how the apostolic teachings were expressed in the New Testament.

The middle way. The second reason why Logos Christology won out over the other options was that it was the only view of Christ that was able to—pardon the colloquialism—have its cake and eat it too. As I have written elsewhere, "Orthodoxy is the middle way between the extreme alternatives."[4] But the "middle way" does not imply a compromise or a median. Rather, it refuses the "either/or" approach of the adoptionists and gnostics in favor of a "both/and" approach. In other words, both adoptionists and gnostics chose one of Christ's two natures to emphasize over the other. On one extreme, the adoptionists affirmed Jesus' human nature while denying or diminishing his divine nature. At the other extreme, the gnostics affirmed the divine nature while denying or diminishing the human nature. We know that part of their motivation for this was to "protect" the immutability and impassibility of the divine from the mutability and passibility of the human. From the perspective of the church fathers,

---

[3]I should not let it go without saying that I personally believe that, above all, Logos Christology won out because it is true and correct and that it was God's will that the Holy Spirit would guide the church to the best interpretation of the person of Christ possible in each generation (Jn 14:26; 16:13).

[4]James L. Papandrea, *Trinity 101: Father, Son, Holy Spirit* (Liguori, MO: Liguori, 2012), 67-69.

the heretics at each extreme favor some biblical passages while ignoring others. For example, the adoptionists used John 14:28 ("the
Father is greater than I") as a favorite prooftext, but they explained
away John 10:30 ("the Father and I are one"). The gnostics (and later,
the modalists) did the opposite.

But orthodoxy, as the church fathers defined it, refuses to choose
some Scriptures at the expense of others. It refuses to ignore a whole
set of Scripture passages to make interpretation of other passages
easier. Rather than ask which of these two passages is true, orthodoxy
accepts the mystery that they are both true and interprets them in
light of each other. Orthodoxy refuses to choose between the two
poles of a false dichotomy, or between the two aspects of a paradox, or
between two apostolic writings or dominical sayings—orthodoxy accepts them and holds them all together.[5]

Embracing this mystery means that when it comes to the divine
and human in the person of Christ, it is not a question of choosing
one over the other or of protecting one from the other. Like the relationship of persons in the Trinity, the relationship of divine and
human in the second person of the Trinity is one of balance—the
balance of unity and distinction.[6] The unity means that the two natures of divinity and humanity are *one* in that they are united in the
one person of Christ without compromising the integrity of each in
any way that would imply that the divine had changed or suffered.
The distinction between the two natures does not go so far as to be a
separation that would destroy the unity of the person Jesus Christ. In
other words, the middle way is not a compromise or a median, but it
is the balance that holds full divinity and full humanity together so
that neither is diminished.[7]

---

[5]For some examples of church fathers who understood orthodoxy to be the middle way be-
tween extreme alternatives, see Clement of Alexandria, *Exhortation to the Greeks* 2; Novatian,
On the Trinity 30.6; Basil of Caesarea, *On the Holy Spirit* 30; Gregory of Nyssa, *On the Holy
Trinity; Catechetical Orations* 1-4 (especially 3); *On Not Three Gods* (where orthodoxy is
described as between adoptionism and tritheism); and Gregory of Nazianzus, *Theological
Orations* 23.8; 30. See also Frances M. Young, with Andrew Teal, *From Nicaea to Chalcedon:
A Guide to the Literature and Its Background* (Grand Rapids: Baker Academic, 2010), 135, 163.
[6]Papandrea, *Trinity 101*, 84-88.
[7]Ibid., 79-84.

As I noted above, we must reject labels of "high christology" and "low christology" as they are sometimes applied to New Testament documents. These labels are at best unhelpful and at worst misleading. The fact that orthodoxy can be described as the middle way between the extreme alternatives only reinforces the observation that the christology that developed from the New Testament documents was neither "high" nor "low" but was in fact in that place of balance that takes seriously both the divinity and the humanity of Christ. A truly "high" christology would be gnosticism, and the New Testament writers that are often labeled "high christology," such as the Johannine writings, were actually refuting the early forms of gnosticism.[8] A truly "low" christology would be adoptionism, and documents such as the Gospel of Mark, which are often labeled with a "low christology," actually affirm the divinity of Christ against adoptionism. Therefore the New Testament writings are neither "high" nor "low" in their christology— they are, in fact, right in the middle—affirming (each in their own way) the Logos Christology of the mainstream church against the extremes on either side. For a visual overview of the way that Logos Christology is the middle way between the extreme alternatives, see the chart titled "Christology Continuum" at the end of the book.

The differences are subtle but significant. In hindsight it may seem as though the five different views of Christ are worlds apart, but in reality the differences might not have been all that clear to many people in the early church. The main points of difference between the five views of Christ revolve around the way each one understands divinity and the way the Creator interacts (or doesn't interact) with creation.

On the one hand, the two variations of adoptionism, along with Logos Christology, accepted the Jewish understanding of divinity, that is, that there is only one divinity, there can be no degrees of divinity, and divinity must be eternal. The two versions of gnosticism, on the other hand, accepted a pagan understanding of divinity in which there were many deities, some of whom were born from the cosmic

---

[8]See, e.g., Jn 20:27 (Thomas touches Jesus' wounds) and 1 Jn 4:2-3 as well as the many times in all the Gospels where we are told that Jesus ate.

procreation of pairs of older deities and who therefore represented lower ranks of divinity.

So when it came to speaking about the "origin" of the Savior, adoptionists, on the one hand, saw his birth as a baby and deduced that therefore he could not be in any way divine. Divinity could not have a beginning to its existence (it could not be "born") and it could not change (i.e., grow up). Whatever divinity (or spiritual entity) was empowering him must therefore be external to his person. Gnostics, on the other hand, saw his miracles and deduced that he must be divine, but they assumed that he must be a lower deity than the Father God he preached. Also, their extreme dualism led them to assume that divinity could not come into contact with the physical world, so they reasoned that he could not really be a human and that any apparent humanity he had was an illusion.

Therefore both the adoptionists and the gnostics separated divinity from humanity in a way that the two substances could not be united in one person. For the adoptionists, the fact that Jesus was "begotten" meant that he was created, either the product of a normal birth from Mary and Joseph or created by God without any part of him that was uncreated. He was the Son of God by adoption but not by nature. For the gnostics, even though he was divine, he could still be created in a sense, and he was begotten in the heavenly realm as part of an extended family of gods.

Only Logos Christology allowed the possibility that the two substances could coexist in one person. For Logos Christology, begetting is not creation but rather something called *generation*, which became a way to talk about how it is that the Logos is also divine without being a second God. He is one divinity with the Father (and the Holy Spirit), but he is not one and the same as the Father (or the Holy Spirit). There is a hierarchy in the Trinity (the Son is the *second person* of the Trinity), but it is not a hierarchy of divinity. All three persons are equal in divinity because they are all the same divinity.[9]

Both adoptionists and gnostics believed in the need for a separation of humanity from divinity. Both were concerned that the

---

[9]Papandrea, *Trinity 101*, 86-88.

suffering of Christ would compromise the immutability and impassibility of the divine, although some of the gnostics were content simply to say that the suffering was all part of the illusion. The mainstream theologians were also aware of the need to preserve the immutability and impassibility of divinity, but they did it in a different way. Rather than make a separation between divinity and humanity in which Jesus (or the Christ) was one or the other, Logos Christology understood a union of the two natures of divinity and humanity in which the integrity of each nature is maintained. The passion affected the human nature only, so the divine nature remained immutable and impassible. Thus while the adoptionists put the whole person of Christ on the creature side of the Creator/creation divide, saying that he was created and therefore not divine, and the gnostics allowed that he could be both created and divine, Logos Christology spoke of the two natures of Christ united in one person, but in a way in which one nature could be divine and uncreated and the other nature could be created and mutable.

It follows, then, that neither the adoptionists nor the gnostics envisioned a Christ in which there was a union of the divine with the human. In Spirit Adoptionism (Christ as prophet), the Holy Spirit *anoints* the mere human known as Jesus, but this is no more of a union of the divine with the human than the prophets enjoyed, even if some of the adoptionists believed that the Holy Spirit is divine. In Angel Adoptionism (Christ as angel), a created spiritual being *indwells* the man Jesus, but only temporarily, and even then it is not a union with the divine per se, only a union with a spiritual entity—a created being inspiring another created being. In Hybrid Gnosticism (Christ as cosmic mind), a quasi-divine being, that is, a lower deity, *inhabits* a quasi-human being, someone taking the form of humanity as a disguise but who is not really human. And in Docetic Gnosticism (Christ as phantom), a quasi-divine being comes as an *apparition* in the *appearance* of humanity, but that humanity is an illusion.

Only Logos Christology is an *incarnation* in which the Word "became flesh," meaning that the divine acquired the human nature and united with it (Jn 1:14).[10] With Logos Christology, there is no time before the union when Jesus is a mere human, because his humanity was created at his conception, which was the moment of union with the divine and preexistent Logos.

With an adoptionist anointing or indwelling, Jesus began as a mere human, and at some point in his adult life he was "adopted" by God, which resulted in spiritual inspiration and empowerment. But he was, in essence, a mere human who was elevated to the status of a prophet who never really united with the divine. In the case of gnostic inhabitation or apparition, the Christ is a divine entity who takes on the form or the appearance of humanity, but he was in essence the opposite of the adoptionist Jesus—he was a divine being who never really united with humanity.

Logos Christology understood the person of Jesus Christ in terms of a descent of the divine Logos, but one that went so far as to actually make contact with humanity and to unite with it. As the church fathers understood it, this allowed the divine nature of Christ to glorify his human nature, which in turn makes it possible for our human nature to be sanctified and ultimately raised. The doctrine of *theosis*, or "deification," is the concept that the incarnation is a "wonderful exchange" in which Christ became like us so that we could become like him (2 Pet 1:3-4). We are the ones adopted and elevated by God, but only because the divine Logos descended to become one of us (Jn 1:12-13). Christ is not adopted, nor does he ascend from mere humanity; rather he descends to humanity (Phil 2:6-8).[11]

To put it simply, in adoptionism Jesus was adopted by God, and we can be too. Just like Jesus, the rest of us can, if we obey God perfectly, ascend to a higher status. In gnosticism, the Christ is divine, and we are too. Just like the Christ, the human soul is a divine spark that descended into the physical world but is essentially disconnected from it, though regular humans are trapped in material bodies. In Logos

---

[10]The language of "becoming" here is not interpreted as though the divine undergoes a change. It simply means that the divine and preexistent Logos became one of us by uniting with flesh (i.e., our human nature).

[11]Papandrea, *Reading the Early Church Fathers*, 141-47.

Christology, Christ was always divine, but he united with humanity, so that we who are human could be raised up to unite with divinity in union with God. He is one of us, but he is unique among us because he descended so that we could ascend.

Thus only Logos Christology has a permanent, ontological union of the human and the divine. This union will later (in the fifth century) come to be called a *hypostatic* union, which can be translated as a *personal* union—the two natures are not kept separate, but are united in the one person of Jesus Christ. Both extremes of adoptionism and gnosticism, however, diminished the union by making it partial and temporary. As we have seen, they apparently felt the need for a strict demarcation between the human person (if there was one) and the spiritual entity that inspired, indwelt or inhabited him. In this they often went so far as to call the human (or tangible) person "Jesus," as distinguished from the spiritual (or divine) entity called "the Christ."

Logos Christology refused to separate Jesus and "the Christ" into two subjects, and Irenaeus in particular criticized the practice. For the mainstream church, Jesus Christ is one person who has two natures. The two natures are distinct enough to maintain the integrity of divine immutability and impassibility, but they are not separate—they are united in one person.

To summarize the differences between the five views of Christ, we could say that for Spirit Adoptionists, the Christ anointed Jesus; for Angel Adoptionists, the Christ indwelt Jesus; for Hybrid Gnostics, the Christ came disguised as Jesus; and for Docetic Gnostics, the Christ appeared, but Jesus was an illusion. When Logos Christology affirms that the Word became flesh, it means that the divine Logos was incarnate and acquired a fully human nature—and unlike the others, this was a permanent union. Divine and human, once united in Christ, would never separate.

CHRISTOLOGY AND SOTERIOLOGY

As I have written elsewhere, there are three observable laws of doctrine in the early church.[12] The first is that *heresy forces orthodoxy to*

---

[12]Papandrea, *Trinity 101*, 73-76.

define itself. Not that heresy precedes orthodoxy, but that in each generation orthodoxy was clarified in opposition to the alternatives. This means that Logos Christology was defined over against adoptionism and gnosticism. The second law is that *orthodoxy is the middle way between the extreme alternatives.* We have seen this to be the case as well, and it is consistent with the early church fathers' understanding of apostolic succession. The third law is that *christology informs soteriology,* meaning that whatever one believes about the Savior will necessarily drive what that person believes about salvation—how the Savior saves.[13]

Adoptionism as a christology assumes that Jesus had to effectively save himself before he could be a Savior. He earned his adoption by his perfect obedience to God. Therefore as a Savior he turns out to be more of a trailblazer than a rescuer. He shows the rest of humanity the way, but each of us must do what he did—achieve perfect obedience and earn the adoption as a child of God. So an adoptionist christology logically leads to a salvation by works.

Gnosticism, on the other hand, is a christology in which the Christ never quite comes down to our level. As is well known, a hallmark of gnosticism is the belief that Christ came to bring "secret knowledge"— probably an awareness of every soul's divinity, among other things. This christology leads to a soteriology in which Christ came to enlighten humanity, not to save humanity—and for most gnostics, he only came to enlighten a select few. Salvation is illumination, because the problem with humanity is not sin; it is ignorance.

The anthropology behind the christology. This shows that underneath each christology is a corresponding anthropology, a particular view of humanity that is also interrelated with a person's beliefs about Christ. For example, the adoptionist christology assumes an anthropology in which sin is a real concern, but perfection is possible. In Augustine's time this type of anthropology would be championed by

---

[13]It can happen that it works the other way around, that a person begins with a certain soteriology and that drives his or her christology. See Charles H. Talbert, *The Development of Christology During the First Hundred Years and Other Essays on Early Christian Christology* (Leiden: Brill, 2011), 4-5, 25.

Pelagius, and it led him to reject the idea that human nature is fallen. For the early adoptionists, they seem to have believed it was possible to follow the whole law perfectly, and anyone who did not had none but themselves to blame. Jesus set the example and taught us everything we need to know to make the right choices, so salvation only requires that we follow his lead and obey God in everything. But mainstream Christians were not so optimistic, and many people rightly worried that if salvation was achieved through obedience (by works), then there was a good chance that they could not ever be obedient enough to earn their salvation.

At the other extreme, gnostic christology assumes an anthropology in which human souls are divine sparks trapped in material bodies. So we are all divine, and our biggest problem is that we don't know it. It was the ultimate version of "I'm okay, you're okay," because humanity was only "fallen" in the literal sense of having fallen from the heavens to the earth. In the gnostic Gospel of Mary, the Savior is recorded as saying, "There is no such thing as sin."[14] Therefore salvation is information. Christ came to bring the knowledge that humans are not really part of creation but can rise above it (and in fact the enlightened ones were meant to rise above the rest of humanity). But most Christians were sufficiently schooled in Jewish monotheism to recognize that such a belief was idolatrous. To say there are many gods was bad enough, but to say that we are gods was not really a viable belief for most Christians.

For Logos Christology, the incarnation of Christ was divine intervention, a rescue mission to save people who could not save themselves. Sin is real, and humanity is fallen, to the extent that we cannot earn our own adoption by God. But we can be adopted by God through identification with his natural Son (Jn 1:10-13). It would not be enough for Christ to bring information or even to set an example. He had to become one of us, and represent us, even on the cross.[15]

If we think of anthropology as defining the problem (what it is

---

[14]Nicola Denzey Lewis, *Introduction to "Gnosticism": Ancient Voices, Christian Worlds* (Oxford: Oxford University Press, 2013), 269.

[15]Papandrea, *Reading the Early Church Fathers*, 219-25.

about humanity that causes us to need salvation) and soteriology as the solution to the problem (what needs to be done to fix what's broken), then christology is both the agent and the method of salvation (who the Savior is and how he accomplished salvation on behalf of humanity). Adoptionism has an optimistic anthropology and a christology in which Jesus is reduced to the one who sets the example, which leads to a soteriology of human effort (works). Gnosticism has an extremely optimistic anthropology and a christology in which the Christ is reduced to a bringer of information, which leads to a soteriology of enlightenment. Logos Christology has a more realistic anthropology and a christology with an ontological union of the divine and the human. As Anselm of Canterbury would later write in *Cur Deus Homo?* (*Why the God-Man?*), the Savior has two natures because both natures are required for salvation. The divine nature of Christ allows him to overcome sin and death through divine intervention, and the human nature of Christ allows him to truly be one of us so that he can represent us on the cross. Therefore Logos Christology leads to a soteriology of atonement (Jesus Christ pays the price for our sin) and also allows for the hope that we as humans can experience union with God in eternal life.

The importance of resurrection. Neither adoptionism nor gnosticism leaves room for *theosis* or in fact for any real union with God. Docetism and gnosticism reject the idea completely, but of course they solved the problem by claiming that human souls are divine to begin with. However, in doing so, they were arguing that we are not really human and that we were never meant to be corporeal beings. For them, all of creation—including the human body—is worthless. In fact, docetics and gnostics, as well as several of the major philosophical schools, taught that the human body was ultimately to be discarded. They believed that the human soul was trapped in the body like a kind of prison, and the afterlife that one hoped for was to shed the body, like a snake sheds its skin, and live as a disembodied spirit. If one could not achieve this, then one would be reincarnated to try again.

On the other hand, the mainstream church taught that creation is good because the Creator is good. Furthermore, the human body is more than simply a part of God's good creation; it is an essential part of humanity. It is not to be discarded in favor of a noncorporeal existence; it is to be redeemed and raised. Who we are as humans includes our bodies.

Of the five views of Jesus Christ in the early church, all but Logos Christology rejected the belief in a bodily resurrection of Christ. Adoptionists apparently taught that the resurrection was a metaphor for eternal life. Docetics and gnostics taught that the resurrection appearances of Christ were either an illusion or the revelation of Christ's true nonhuman nature. Only Logos Christology affirmed the bodily resurrection of Christ, and this doctrine was so important to the early church that it made its way into the creed. It was important because mainstream Christians believed that Jesus' resurrection foreshadowed our own resurrection and made it possible.[16]

Therefore the adoptionists' hope for the afterlife was probably no different from the pre-Christian Jewish hope of going to be with one's ancestors. The gnostic hope was to effectively shed any remnant of humanity: to be no longer human and no longer embodied. The orthodox Christian hope is to be fully human and embodied but glorified and perfected. The belief in the resurrection of the body dignifies humanity and requires us to respect the bodies of other people. Rejecting the bodily resurrection of Jesus Christ, and rejecting the belief in the resurrection in general, leads to the denigration of the human body and the erroneous assumption that we can be human apart from our bodies—or worse, that the human body is something that is corrupted or disposable.

In each chapter I have pointed to the ways in which a particular christology might direct believers to one kind of lifestyle or another. We can see now that docetism and gnosticism, with their disregard for creation, can lead to the denigration of the human body, and this is quite consistent with the charge of the early church fathers that the docetics and gnostics did not care for the poor. It should go without

---

[16]For the apologists' arguments in favor of resurrection against philosophical views of the afterlife, see Justin Martyr, *On the Resurrection*; and Athenagoras, *On the Resurrection of the Dead*. See also Papandrea, *Reading the Early Church Fathers*, 37-42.

saying that they also did not care for the environment. However, we have also seen that while the docetics and adherents of Docetic Gnosticism were led by their dualism into an ascetic lifestyle, Hybrid Gnosticism apparently led its followers into a hedonistic lifestyle based on the idea that the tangible world was useful as a means to an end but ultimately not valued. So on the gnostic side, depending on whether they believed the Christ shunned the material world or used it as a disguise, members of the gnostic factions either denied their own bodies or indulged them. On the adoptionist side, it is probably the case that members of those factions leaned toward asceticism, as we can see in some of the documents known as the apocryphal acts.[17] In the mainstream church, Logos Christology led the majority of Christians to look for a middle way with regard to lifestyle as well—neither abusing the body nor indulging it. Of course there were ascetics within the christological mainstream, but the church at large did not endorse extreme versions of asceticism that punished the body or required celibacy of all members.

There is also evidence that the christologies informed different views of the sacraments. Some adoptionists and some docetics rejected the use of wine in the Eucharist, presumably because the adoptionists did not believe that Jesus' blood had any atoning significance and because the docetics did not believe he had any blood. In both cases they apparently substituted water for the wine, a practice now called *aquarianism*. Some of the gnostics may have rejected the sacraments altogether, but it seems that those who held to a Hybrid Gnostic christology had a eucharistic ritual that was presented like a kind of magic trick, in which a small cup is poured out and fills up a larger cup.[18]

When it comes to baptism, it seems that Docetic Gnosticism led its followers to reject baptism completely because of its connection to creation—the water and the flesh.[19] On the other hand, Hybrid Gnosticism had its own baptism ritual, another magic trick in which fire supposedly appeared on the surface of the baptismal water.[20]

---

[17]Papandrea, *Reading the Early Church Fathers*, 82-87.
[18]Irenaeus of Lyons, *Against Heresies* 1.13.2.
[19]Irenaeus of Lyons, *Against Heresies* 1.21.1.
[20]*On Rebaptism* 16-17.

We might summarize the connection between christology and life-style as follows. Adoptionists refused to worship Christ because they did not believe he was divine, and therefore they believed that worshiping him would be a form of idolatry. They had an optimistic anthropology that allowed them to believe that human perfection was possible, but since they believed that salvation required following Jesus' example of obedience to God, they probably emphasized asceticism, and some even required celibacy of all adherents.

Docetics and gnostics had no problem with worshiping Christ, but they also worshiped themselves, believing that they were essentially divine and that there was no such thing as sin. Some of them (Docetic Gnostics) shunned the material world and the human body through lives of asceticism and celibacy, though they also apparently ignored the poor and refused to engage in society in any positive way. Others (Hybrid Gnostics) believed that the material world could be used with no detriment to the soul, and so they lived hedonistic lives, often rejecting childbearing while embracing promiscuity. Because they believed Christ had taught them that they too were divine, theirs was a self-centered christology.

The Legacy of Adoptionism: Arianism

As adoptionism evolved into the fourth century, the idea of the adoption of Jesus as an elevation of status, combined with the universal acceptance of the prologue to the Gospel of John as a description of a preexistent Logos, led to a new kind of adoption, one in which the elevation of status was extended into the divine realm. In other words, in the fourth century we see a new kind of adoptionism in which it was believed that Jesus was rewarded with divinity. He still begins as a mere human, but as a result of his perfect obedience to God, his adoption made him quasi-divine, that is, divine but not as divine as the Father.

In around the year 319, an Alexandrian priest named Arius was teaching that Jesus was adopted by God and granted the indwelling, not of an angel, but of the preexistent Logos. According to Arius, however, his Logos was not to be thought of as *eternally* preexistent, since he was still created—just created before the rest of creation. Arius had made a concession to the mainstream belief in the preexistence of the Logos but could not accept his full divinity, so he solved his problem by bringing in the pagan concept of degrees of divinity. Thus his Jesus could be elevated to a quasi-divine status without being thought of as eternally divine or fully divine (as divine as the Father).

Much has been written on the background of Arianism, some even claiming that it is not really a form of adoptionism. However, it is clear that, as a christology of ascent, Arianism was built on the foundation laid in the second and third centuries by both Spirit Adoptionism and Angel Adoptionism. In other words, Arianism is a christology in which *humanity acquires divinity*, as opposed to Logos Christology, in which *divinity acquires humanity*.

However, we can also find precedents for Arianism within a few of the mainstream theologians of the second and third centuries. For example, Theophilus of Antioch (bishop 168–188) described the Logos in ways that implied Christ had a beginning to his existence.[21] Theophilus used the analogy of a spoken word to explain the Logos, the Word of God. In his christology, the Logos was at first only a thought in the mind of God with no eternal existence distinct from the Father—as if to say that in the beginning, the Word was "in" God but was not yet "with" God. This may have allowed Theophilus's successors in Antioch to believe that the Logos had no existence as distinct from the Father until he was "spoken forth" or "emitted" from the Father. This allowed Paul of Samosata (bishop of Antioch from 260 to 268) to teach that the Logos existed only in the mind of God—in foreknowledge but not in substance—until the time at which he was created by the Father. Thus both the Spirit Adoptionism of Paul of Samosata and the Angel Adoptionism of Lucian of Antioch (lead catechist there during the episcopate of Paul) could find their origin in Theophilus.

Others, including the Alexandrian Origen (lead catechist in Alexandria 204–215) and the early Dionysius of Alexandria (bishop 247–264),

---

[21]On the christology of Theophilus of Antioch, see James L. Papandrea, *Novatian of Rome and the Culmination of Pre-Nicene Orthodoxy*, Princeton Theological Monographs 175 (Eugene, OR: Pickwick, 2011), 11-15.

have left writings that could have contributed to the development of Arianism.[22] However, it seems that there was a strain of thought in Antioch, coming originally from Theophilus, that led to Arius. And although Theophilus's writings were never declared heresy, later Western writers such as Irenaeus, Tertullian, Hippolytus and Novatian would progressively correct his understanding of the Logos.[23]

Arius, however, did not follow the trajectory that would lead to Nicaea; instead he reasoned that if both the Father and the Son were equally divine, that would make two Gods (as he expressed it, they would be brothers, not Father and Son). Accepting the idea that a being can be both divine and created allowed him to see the Son of God as being somewhere in between humanity and divinity rather than both fully human and fully divine. This led to an Arian view of the Trinity in which there was a hierarchy of divinity and a separation between the Father and Son—the separation of Creator and creature. This, in turn, led the mainstream bishops and theologians to affirm the consubstantiality of the Father and Son.

THE LEGACY OF GNOSTICISM: MODALISM

By the fourth century, gnosticism had become something other than Christian, even taking the word "Christian" in the broadest sense. This was probably true even earlier, but certainly by the fourth century the gnostics had separated from the mainstream church, written their own gospels in opposition to the canonical Gospels and the apostles of the mainstream, and had become a different religion altogether. Probably the most discernable version of gnosticism after this final split with the mainstream was Manichaeism. Therefore gnosticism did not continue to evolve as a heresy within the church as adoptionism did. However, already in the early third century we can see another heresy taking its place as the christology that diminished the humanity of Jesus, and that was modalism.

As I indicated above, modalism is not a christology, strictly speaking, but rather a way of understanding the Trinity. However, the modalist

---

[22]See Papandrea, *Reading the Early Church Fathers*, 111-15, 141-47.
[23]Papandrea, *Novatian of Rome*, 19-46, 73-105.

understanding of the Trinity claimed that the Father and the Son were one and the same, which effectively left no room for any real humanity in the Son.[24] Therefore modalism is the legacy of gnosticism, not in the sense that gnosticism evolved into modalism (it didn't), but in the sense that modalism took gnosticism's place as the view of Christ that affirmed his divinity but denied his humanity.[25] The biggest difference between gnosticism and modalism is that gnosticism is built on a foundation of dualism while modalism is built on a foundation of monism.[26]

In fact, whereas Docetic Gnosticism said that Christ's humanity was an illusion and Hybrid Gnosticism said that Christ's humanity was a disguise, modalism claimed that the Son was the Father in disguise and his humanity (including his passion) was an illusion. Thus the modalist Son becomes nothing more than another name for the Father, or a name for the activity of the Father, concepts we can see in some forms of gnosticism.[27] In the Gospel of Thomas, the Son is called the name of the Father.[28] In the Trimorphic Protennoia, the Son of Man is the Father, and says, "I am the Father of everyone."[29] In the Second Treatise of the Great Seth, the Son is identified with the Father.[30] In the Gospel of Truth, the Son is the name of the Father and was the Father coming forth from himself. In the Apocryphon of John, the Son is an aspect of the Father and is also called Father and Mother.[31]

Thus the modalist view of the Trinity, in which the Father, Son and Holy Spirit were one and the same—three names for one person,

---

[24]Hippolytus, *Refutation of All Heresies* 9.5. See Papandrea, *Reading the Early Church Fathers*, 140.

[25]On modalism, see Papandrea, *Reading the Early Church Fathers*, 139-41; and Papandrea, *Trinity 101*, 77-79.

[26]Hippolytus, *Refutation of All Heresies* 9.2-5; *Against Noetus* 1; 7. See Papandrea, *Reading the Early Church Fathers*, 105-8, 140.

[27]J. Zandee, "Gnostic Ideas on the Fall and Salvation," *Numen* 11, no. 1 (1964): 53, 55.

[28]Gospel of Thomas 38-39.

[29]Trimorphic Protennoia 53.

[30]Second Treatise of the Great Seth 59.

[31]Lewis, *Introduction to "Gnosticism,"* 154. However, note that on the same page Lewis erroneously ascribes modalist tendencies to the mainstream church when she incorrectly describes consubstantiality in terms of the Son being "identical with" the Father. She is also quite incorrect when she says that a two-natured christology did not develop until the fifth century, as anyone who has read the primary sources knows.

rather than the orthodox three persons in one substance—led to a christology in which the humanity of Jesus was an illusion.

THE LEGACY OF LOGOS CHRISTOLOGY: THE *COMMUNICATIO IDIOMATUM*

Both forms of adoptionism and both forms of gnosticism answer Jesus' question, "Who do you say that I am?" by separating Jesus from the spiritual entity that anointed, indwelt, inhabited or disguised itself with him. In other words "Jesus" was one being and "the Christ" was another. But Irenaeus of Lyons recognized the problem with this separation and warned against it.[32] He knew that separating the human from the divine in that way would rob humanity of its hope of union with God. Both extremes of adoptionism and gnosticism had tried to protect the divine from contact with suffering, but in doing so they also "protected" humanity from contact with the divine. As the mainstream church would eventually clarify through the ecumenical councils, the union of human and divine in Jesus Christ is a *hypostatic*, or personal, union—a permanent, ontological union in which the divine glorifies the human, which in turn allows for the sanctification and glorification of humanity in general.

The *communicatio idiomatum* is the communication of idiomatic properties in the person of Christ. This means that what is natural to the human nature is communicated to the divine nature, and what is natural for the divine nature is communicated to the human nature. Specifically, the suffering and solidarity with humanity that is natural to Jesus' human nature is communicated to the divine nature, so that the divine nature can experience the human condition and embody compassion for humanity while at the same time remaining immutable and impassible. In the same way, the incorruptibility and immortality that is natural to the divine nature is communicated to the human nature, glorifying the humanity. This is good news, since our shared human nature means that our own humanity can now also be sanctified and glorified in the resurrection. Because his divinity raised his humanity, our humanity can also be raised.

---

[32]Irenaeus of Lyons, *Against Heresies* 3.9.3; 3.11.7. See Papandrea, *Novatian of Rome*, 24.

However, to separate "Jesus" from "the Christ," as the adoptionists and gnostics did, removed any hope of union with God, because it removed the union of the human with the divine in Jesus Christ. The unity of the person of Christ is important for our union with the divine, and the hypostatic union and the *communicatio idiomatum* are the nexus of contact between humanity and God. Without that union, humanity has no hope of salvation. We can try to earn our salvation, as adoptionist christology implies we must, but we will never ascend to God. We can try to become enlightened, as gnostic christology implies we must, but the divine will never descend to make contact with us. The Mediator cannot be human only or divine only, or even somewhere in between human and divine, as in Arianism. The Mediator must be both human and divine—truly human as we are, and fully divine as the Father is—or salvation itself is an illusion.

As we have now seen, every generation of the church's history had an expression of christology that was consistent with the teachings of the apostles—this was Logos Christology. And although every generation also had its versions of adoptionism and gnosticism (and then modalism), it was clear to the majority that Logos Christology was the orthodox christology as opposed to the alternatives at the extremes. Therefore, as I have already noted above, there is no need to speak of "proto-orthodoxy" as if there was no true orthodoxy before the ecumenical councils. In fact apostolic succession proves that there was. Just as the orthodox understanding of the Trinity was one of a balance of unity and distinction of the three persons, so also the orthodox understanding of the second person was one of a balance of unity and distinction of the two natures. The humanity and divinity in the person of Christ are unified in a permanent, ontological union that maintains the integrity of the singular subject who is the person of Jesus Christ. The two natures are one in the sense that they are inseparable. At the same time, the two natures are distinct in that they maintain their own integrity and so that the divine remains immutable and impassible. They are distinct but not separate. They are one but not confused or mixed together in any way that would diminish either nature.

Two Final Caveats: Modern Docetism and Modern Adoptionism

There is a functional docetism alive and well in the church of the twenty-first century. Most people, if asked what they think the afterlife will be like, would reply that their soul will leave their body and will live on forever as a pure spirit. Many, if not most, Christians probably envision life in heaven as a purely spiritual (i.e., incorporeal) existence. However, that is not what the New Testament or the church fathers taught. We do not expect to be rid of our bodies forever—that was the hope of the gnostics and some of the philosophers. We hope to be reunited with our bodies in the resurrection. We expect to live eternally with resurrection bodies, which, while raised and glorified, will still be in some way consistent with the bodies we have now (1 Cor 15). We may not understand it any more than a caterpillar understands what it's like to be a butterfly, but this is what we believe, and this is what we hope for. Therefore, we must be careful that we do not perpetuate the docetic view of the afterlife, because that leads to a disregard for the body, for the bodies of others and even for creation in general.

At the other extreme, the adoptionist separation of "Jesus" from "the Christ" finds expression in contemporary scholarship, most notably in some forms of liberation theology, and in the so-called quest for the historical Jesus.[33] Whether one begins with an adoptionist christology or with the separation of the "historical Jesus" from "the Christ of faith," this separation leads to the loss of the divinity of Christ, the loss of the atonement and the loss of the union of humanity with the divine. The rejection of the bodily resurrection of Christ (along with his virgin birth and miracles) is another characteristic of this kind of contemporary adoptionism, and as we have seen, this in turn leads to the loss of humanity's hope of resurrection. The problem is recognized by contemporary adoptionists, but rather than hold on to the atonement, and to avoid the salvation by works inherent in adoptionism, proponents of this school of thought will usually simply

---

[33]For an excellent response to quest scholarship, see Luke Timothy Johnson, *The Real Jesus: The Misguided Quest for the Historical Jesus and the Truth of the Traditional Gospels* (San Francisco: HarperSanFrancisco, 1997).

resort to universalism.[34] One can understand the attraction of universalism. Personally, I would love to be a universalist—it would be much easier, and much more comfortable—but I cannot be a universalist, mainly because Jesus was not a universalist.[35]

Modern adoptionism diminishes the role of Christ in favor of a human-centered, present-oriented definition of salvation. In other words, sin is defined narrowly as oppression, and salvation is defined as liberation from oppression. Often tradition—especially the church's tradition—is associated with oppression, so that it is also implied that salvation is a liberation from tradition. However, to be liberated from tradition is to be left with an empty relativism, in which Anselm's understanding of the atonement is traded for Abelard's intentionalism.[36] Then Jesus as Savior is reduced to just a good example to follow, and the cross becomes nothing more than the unfortunate fate of one man who tried to buck the system.

In fact, some will go so far as to say that Jesus must have sinned like the rest of us because (they reason) sin is part of humanity, and if he didn't sin, then he wasn't really human. In this way they emphasize Jesus' humanity to the detriment of his divinity and his identity as the second person of the Trinity. We have seen that the human body is an essential part of our humanity—this is true. But it is not true that sin is an essential part of our humanity. The truth is that when we sin, we fall short of our true humanity, and so Jesus Christ's sinlessness actually means that he realized his full humanity more than the rest of us. But contemporary adoptionism often attempts to let people off the hook for personal sin while redefining sin only in terms of injustice.

Therefore we must also be careful that we do not accept this new form of adoptionism just because it is promoted by scholars. By separating the human Jesus from "the Christ of faith" they have removed

---

[34]Recent years have seen a vigorous debate over the validity of universalism. In my opinion, the best, most balanced answer to the question is Hans Urs von Balthasar's *Dare We Hope "That All Men Be Saved"?*, trans. David Kipp and Lothar Krauth (San Francisco: Ignatius, 1988).

[35]See the teachings of Jesus in which someone is separated from God in the afterlife, such as the parable of the rich man and Lazarus (Lk 16:19-31) and the parable of the wedding banquet (Mt 22:1-14, esp. Mt 22:11-14).

[36]Papandrea, *Reading the Early Church Fathers*, 219-24.

the very elements of Christianity that require faith to believe. In fact, all versions of the adoptionist and docetic heresies have, by diminishing either the divinity or the humanity of Christ, effectively diminished humanity's hope of any union with God. Only Logos Christology—and its legacy, Nicene theology—takes sin seriously enough to be realistic about human nature, offering humanity the hope of reconciliation with God that results in eternal life.

	Christ as Prophet *Spirit Adoptionism*	Christ as Angel *Angel Adoptionism*	Christ as Word *Logos Christology*	Christ as Cosmic Mind *Hybrid Gnosticism*	Christ as Phantom *Docetic Gnosticism*
Separates Jesus from "the Christ"?	Yes	Yes	No	Yes	Yes (because there is no Jesus)
Jesus is:	A mere human	A mere human	Jesus Christ is one person with two natures: truly human and fully divine	A tangible being with a "luminous" or "ethereal" body, but not really human	An illusion—he had no body at all
The Christ is:	A title for the anointed Jesus	A created, spiritual being indwelling Jesus		A lesser deity disguised as a human	A lesser deity who appeared to be human
The Son is:	The one who earned the anointing and the title "Christ" through obedience to God's law	The one who earned the indwelling of the angel through obedience to God's law	The Logos, the preexistent Second Person of the Trinity and the divine nature of Jesus Christ	The offspring of a pair of gods in a polytheistic pantheon	The offspring of a pair of gods in a polytheistic pantheon
Bodily resurrection?	No	No	Yes	No	No
Virgin birth?	No	Yes	Yes	No birth at all	No birth at all
Union of human with the spiritual?	Anointing (not a true union)	Indwelling (temporary union with a spiritual entity, but not a union with the divine)	Incarnation (permanent union of the divine and human)	Inhabitation (no union, just a temporary disguise)	Apparition (no union, just a temporary illusion)
Lifestyle	Legalism, some asceticism	Legalism, some asceticism	Balanced lifestyle: not to punish the body or to indulge it	Hedonism	Asceticism

Subject Index

Scripture Index

OTHER BOOKS BY JAMES PAPANDREA

*The Adventures of the Space Boys: The Space Boys
Meet the Moon Bully* (with Joe Groshek)

*Handed Down: The Catholic Faith
of the Early Christians*

*Novatian of Rome and the Culmination
of Pre-Nicene Orthodoxy*

*Reading the Early Church Fathers:
From the Didache to Nicaea*

Rome: A Pilgrim's Guide to the Eternal City

*Seven Revolutions: How Christianity Changed the World
and Can Change It Again* (with Mike Aquilina)

*Spiritual Blueprint:
How We Live, Work, Love, Play, and Pray*

Trinity 101: Father, Son, Holy Spirit

*The Wedding of the Lamb: A Historical Approach
to the Book of Revelation*

Finding the Textbook You Need

The IVP Academic Textbook Selector
is an online tool for instantly finding the IVP books
suitable for over 250 courses across 24 disciplines.

ivpacademic.com